The Internet

The Internet

A Practical Guide for Beginners

Keith Fong

The Internet: A Practical Guide for Beginners
1st Edition

Illustrations by Joshua Kwan
Edited by Eldes Tran
Layout by Awadhesh Yadav
Published by Fong Pak Hung
Published in Hong Kong

ISBN: 978-988-76209-0-7

Contents

Acknowledgments

There are many people I'd like to thank for making this book happen.

Firstly my wife, Nicole, for all of your love and support throughout. Thank you for encouraging me to pursue a longtime dream and giving the draft a critical eye as it neared completion.

My parents, Kenny and Jessie, for nurturing my sense of curiosity and for always giving me the love and freedom to pursue whatever I wanted. Thank you both.

My sister, Jacqueline. I've always been proud of and impressed by your art, and I hope this book encourages you to keep pursuing the things you love.

Professor Lawrence Yeung, for your top-notch teaching and guidance in ICOM 6012, and for taking time out of your schedule to help an ex-student with his pet project.

Dr. Pete Membrey, for superbly insightful edits and comments throughout, continually challenging me to make this book more reader friendly, and giving me some great advice for publishing.

Leo W., for being the first reviewer of this book, offering your unparalleled expertise on blockchain (and everything else, really), and answering round after round of questions.

Fionn F., for helping me understand the trickier concepts in this book, giving excellent pointers on the images, and answering round after round of questions.

Jidesh V., for sense-checking the veracity of key points and making sure I cross my T's and dot my I's.

Josh K., for your incredible illustrations and even more incredible patience, working through multiple iterations of each graphic, and not letting glitchy Google Meet calls get in the way of our catch-ups.

Eldes T., for your comprehensive edits and guidance on formatting and publication. Thank you also for introducing me to Scribus and making this book much more readable than it otherwise would be.

Awadhesh Y., for laying this book out and being a top professional throughout. I'm very glad we got to work together.

Roberta B., Justina C., Laura P., Candice A., and Cedric M., for inspiring me with your own passion projects. Roberta, for transforming your passion for dance into a career. We always hear about people taking the leap to chase their dreams and I'm so happy I know someone who's living that out. Justina, for your delightful comics (and knitting and writing and songwriting!). Peggy Pointer may be all the rage for other people, but I think the world could use a little more Underwear Tiger. Laura, with your beautiful paintings and prints. As someone who would struggle to even finish a coloring book, I'm always amazed to see the ideas you bring to life with a paintbrush and watercolors. Candice, with your social work initiatives and the cheer you bring to those around you. Emphasizing and affirming are hard things to master, but I think I speak for many when I say you do them really well. Cedric, with your game design, art, and (so many) memes. My daily productivity would probably be a lot higher in a world where I didn't know you, but you make living in this one just a bit more funny. Just a bit though. :howdy:

Introduction

This book was written to be a beginner's first book on the Internet. It's meant to give interested readers the foundation they need to "speak Internet" and be a basis for further learning and research.

As an undergraduate student, I did not study a STEM subject and occasionally wished I had more of a technical background when I began my professional career. In many ways, this is the sort of book I would've loved to have access to all those years ago.

In that spirit, this book is designed to give a succinct but comprehensive treatment of "must-know" Internet topics. We begin with a brief history of the Internet, looking at the motivations that birthed this transformative technology and some key milestones to date. Chapter 2 is a crash course on computer networking and the basic architecture of the Internet. We explore some of the rationale behind its design and look at what happens under the hood when you access a simple web page. Chapter 3 is an introduction to mobile Internet access and the five generations of mobile Internet technology.

Chapter 4 is on Internet security. We begin with the fundamentals of security and cryptography before diving into common attacks and how to defend against them. This part of the book also introduces concepts needed to understand Chapter 5, which is a primer on blockchain and its many applications. Chapter 6 is about the Internet of Things, cloud computing, and what might happen in a future where more devices are going online and "talking" to one another. Chapter 7 concludes the book with a selection of the most popular questions about the Internet.

Beyond giving definitions to Internet buzzwords, I've tried to outline the principles underpinning the Internet and give practical advice where possible, particularly in the chapter on security.

I hope you'll find this book informative, useful, and not a total bore to read. If you'd like to tell me what you think, do drop me an email at keithfph@gmail.com. You can also find me online at https://keithfph.github.io/.

1

A Brief History of the Internet

The Internet is the largest engineered system in human history. Today, it connects the world by enabling computers, smartphones, game consoles, and countless other devices to communicate with one another using common standards.

After decades of evolution, the Internet is now a vital part of everyday life. We use the Internet to chat with friends across the globe, watch our favorite shows, and shop while we're out and about. Strange as it may sound, the Internet was not designed to be used as it is today.

The precursor to the Internet, ARPANET (the Advanced Research Projects Agency Network), was proposed in the late 1960s. ARPANET was developed for researchers from various university campuses to exchange resources. The success of ARPANET and the emergence of various networks in the '70s led to the need for accepted standards—a "common language" for machines in different locations to "speak" and share information with one another.

In this chapter, we take a quick tour through the history of computer networking, from the birth of packet-switched networks to today's Internet.

What is a computer?

In 1943, a man made one of the worst predictions in history.

Thomas Watson, the then-president of IBM, estimated the world would only need "maybe five computers." With the benefit of hindsight, we can see Watson was only off by a few billion!

Put simply, a computer is a machine that stores and processes information. It takes inputs, stores them in memory, and processes the inputs to give outputs. A computer program is a set of instructions that tells a computer what operations to perform. It tells the computer how to manipulate the inputs it has received and what outputs to produce.

In today's computers, the core programs are referred to as the **operating system (OS)**. The OS dictates how your computer handles input, output, storage, and processing. Applications are run on top of (and built on) the OS.

If that was all a computer was, it would still be a highly complex and incredible machine. However, one of the key components on every modern computing device is the **network interface card (NIC)**. Also called the network adapter, this is a circuit board or chip that enables a computer to communicate with other devices over a local area network (see Chapter 2) or the wider Internet.

If the NIC is the "voice box," then the standardized protocols are the "language" spoken by computers across the Internet. We will be exploring these protocols in detail in the next chapter.

Before the 1960s

Prior to the 1960s, the telephone network was the world's dominant communication network. The telephone system is a type of **circuit-switched network**—a complete point-to-point circuit set aside for two parties to communicate. Over the course of communication, the circuit and all of its bandwidth ("bandwidth" being the maximum amount of data that can be transmitted over the circuit at a time) is reserved for the end users. Circuit-switched networks made sense for telephony as there is usually a constant rate of (voice) data transmitted from the sender to the receiver.

Example of a circuit-switched network

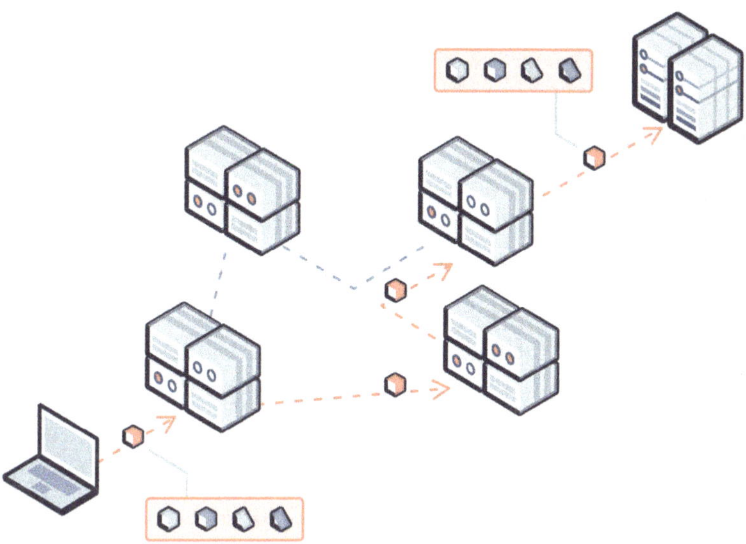

The drawback of circuit-switched networks is wasted capacity. Because circuits are reserved for the entire communication session, they are idle when nothing is sent. This makes circuit-switched networks a very inefficient (and expensive) way to transmit uneven, "bursty" traffic (say, modern Internet traffic). You might use a burst of bandwidth to download a web page or a video file, but the circuit would sit mostly unused while you consumed the content. Though inefficient, this was how the earliest computer networks were implemented, until a monumental change happened in the '60s.

1961–1972: The emergence of packet-switched networks

1961
Leonard Kleinrock publishes work on packet-switched networks.

1969
The first message is sent on ARPANET.

In 1961, Leonard Kleinrock, a graduate student at MIT, published a paper on **packet-switched networks**. In a packet-switched network, messages are first cut up into smaller packets and then sent into the network. Unlike circuit-switched networks, there are no reserved communication links, so messages can be sent across any available path. It's even possible for parts of the same message to travel along different paths before reassembling at the destination. Kleinrock's work was significant for showing how packet switching was more efficient and effective for transmitting irregular, bursty traffic than circuit switching.

Example of a packet-switched network

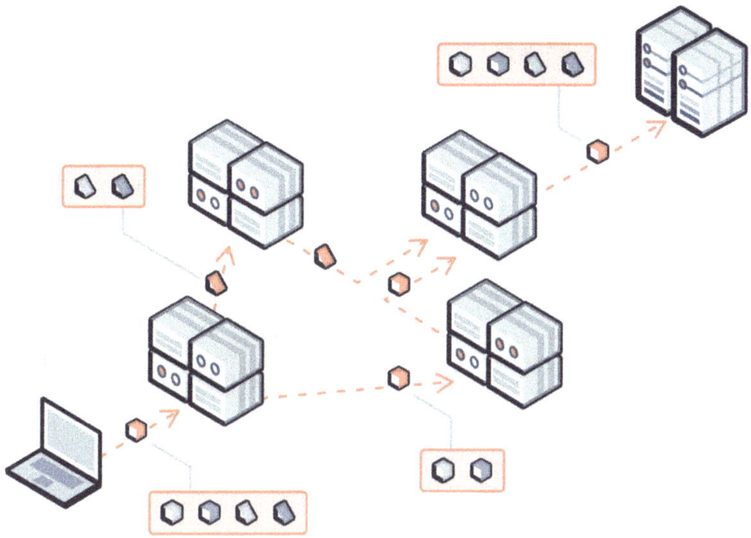

Soon after Kleinrock's paper was published, other research groups began to work on packet-switched networks. In 1964, projects to adapt packet-switched networks for military use began. Five years later, **ARPANET**—the first packet-switched network—was born.

The plan for ARPANET was published in 1967 by Lawrence Roberts, a colleague of Kleinrock's at MIT. After two years of development, Kleinrock supervised the installation of the first ARPANET node at UCLA, with three nodes located at Stanford; the University of Utah; and the University of California, Santa Barbara. For the first ARPANET message, Kleinrock's team intended to send the word "login" to the receiving node at the Stanford Research Institute. The team successfully sent the first two letters before the third caused the computer at the SRI to crash! "Lo" and behold, the ancestor of today's Internet was born.

1972-1989: The development of the modern Internet

1973
Ethernet is invented.

1974
TCP is invented.

1983
The birthday of the Internet: ARPANET and the Defense Data Network change to the TCP/IP standard.

1984
DNS is invented.

By 1972, the number of ARPANET nodes had grown from four to 15. Robert Kahn, an electrical engineer who would later work on the groundbreaking famous TCP and IP protocols, gave the first public demonstration of ARPANET at the International Conference on Computer Communication. The event was a big success and, in Kahn's words, "made the world take notice of packet switching." In the same year, the first device-to-device protocol between ARPANET nodes, the Network Control Protocol (NCP), was completed. As the 1970s progressed, other networks like ALOHANET, Telenet, Cyclades, and Tymnet emerged.

Despite its early success, ARPANET was a single, closed network. In the following years, attempts were made to connect devices besides computer terminals. In 1973, Bob Metcalfe invented the **Ethernet** protocol. Ethernet made it possible to create wire-based networks and connected devices like computers, printers, and shared disks. This development paved the way for modern **local area networks (LANs)**.

In 1974, Robert Kahn and Vinton Cerf laid the foundations for "internetting" (creating a network of networks) by designing the **Transmission Control Protocol (TCP)**. The goal was to allow different packet-switched networks to "talk" to one another, regardless of the software and hardware used in the individual networks. TCP (then called the Transmission Control *Program*) originally handled both the routing of messages to their destinations and ensured messages were delivered reliably. However, out of a desire to keep the two functions separate (and increase scalability), the **Internet Protocol (IP)** was later introduced to handle routing. Reliable data transfer remained the focus of TCP. A few years later, the need for unreliable data transfer (yes, unreliable data transfer) led to the introduction of the **User Datagram Protocol (UDP)**. These three protocols will be covered in the next chapter.

By 1980, TCP/IP was adopted by the U.S. Department of Defense as the standard communications protocol for the Defense Data Network. This proved crucial in accelerating adoption of TCP/IP, as it was a stamp of approval from the world's largest computing organization at the time. Three years later, TCP/IP was officially deployed as the standard host protocol for ARPANET. This saw other protocols (like ARPANET's NCP) fade into obscurity. In fact, January 1, 1983, the day ARPANET and the Defense Data Network changed to the TCP/IP standard, is often remembered as the birthday of the Internet.

Another important component of the Internet arrived in 1984: the **Domain Name System (DNS)** (see Chapter 2). Invented by Paul Mockapetris, DNS translates human-readable domain names (e.g., www.google.com) into structured, numerical IP addresses (e.g., 66.102.10.255). This was a crucial development that changed the

Internet from a tool used by academics into a service that could be used by ordinary people for everyday purposes.

With the foundations of the modern Internet in place, and with the development of powerful microprocessors, computer systems now had the chance to move from "fat client" setups (where all of a user's files were stored locally on the machine) toward client-server architectures. Instead of storing everything on their computer, a user can now request the files they need and decide whether to store it. Perhaps the most famous example of client-server computing was the Internet's next "killer app"—the **World Wide Web**. Where the world once relied on static publications like books and newspapers, the Web paved the way for something revolutionary: a dynamic, "living," and unlimited portal of information.

The 1990s: The birth of the World Wide Web

1989
World Wide Web is invented.

1995
Operation of the Internet backbone is turned over to commercial Internet service providers.

Like the Internet before it, the Web was motivated by academic needs. Tim Berners-Lee, a British scientist working at CERN in the mid-1980s, saw the staggering amounts of data produced by the world's largest particle physics laboratory and imagined an efficient new way for researchers around the globe to share information.

Taking the concept of hypertext (text that contains links to other texts) and using the TCP/IP and DNS protocols, Berners-Lee proposed the World Wide Web in 1989. The Web would be a service that runs on the existing Internet infrastructure, linking textual documents written in **HyperText Markup Language (HTML)**. To make his idea a reality, Berners-Lee and his team developed early versions of HTML, the web browser, the web server, and the **Hypertext Transfer Protocol (HTTP)**. HTTP is the set of rules that web browsers and servers must obey to communicate.

After two years of work by Berners-Lee's team, the World Wide Web was made publicly available on August 6, 1991. For most people, the Web became their first taste of the Internet, opening up new worlds of information, entertainment, and commerce. The introduction of graphical web browsers (like Mosaic in 1993) further sped up Web adoption by presenting attractive, multimedia content to everyday users.

By the mid-1990s, we had reached the beginnings of e-commerce. The National Science Foundation, the creator of NSFNET (the successor of ARPANET in 1990), opened up its network to commercial use in 1991. But after four years, the agency decommissioned NSFNET and turned over operations of the Internet backbone to **Internet service providers (ISPs)** like AT&T and Sprint.

The Internet witnessed explosive growth in the second half of the 1990s. Innovations like Instant Messaging (IM), Peer-to-Peer (P2P) file sharing, and Internet banking transformed the way people lived and worked. As the Internet grew in popularity, Internet companies sprang up left and right and made initial public offerings before they were profitable.

The good times would not last, as the continual speculation eventually led to the infamous dot-com bust in early 2000. While many companies were forced to shut down in the aftermath, companies like Google, Amazon, Yahoo!, and eBay emerged as winners. Key to their success was the expanded reach afforded by the Internet. In a pre-Internet world, only the biggest of companies would have the resources and know-how to operate globally. With the Internet, smaller companies could now sell to a global audience they were previously unable to reach. This is central to the business models of companies like Etsy and Amazon, which would otherwise not have access to a big enough customer base to make their operations profitable.

The 2000s: Going wireless, blockchain, and the cloud

2007
Introduction of the iPhone.

2009
Creation of Bitcoin.

Steve Jobs' introduction of the iPhone in 2007 was the biggest Internet milestone of the 2000s. Up to this point, people largely accessed the Internet from stationary terminals. The iPhone changed all of that by packing the computing power of a desktop computer into a handheld device, accessed via a simple but elegant interface. Together with advances in end-user Internet access, mobile Internet access would soon become commonplace. By 2009, smartphones gave millions of people around the world the ability to enjoy the Web wherever they were.

Two other Internet technologies proposed in the '90s gained widespread adoption by the end of the 2000s. **Blockchain** (see Chapter 5), designed to be a permanent ledger for timestamping documents, became popular with the rise of Bitcoin, the world's first cryptocurrency to solve the double-spending problem. The **cloud** (see Chapter 6) introduced a new computing model, enabling users to access software, storage, and development resources on demand over the Internet.

The 2010s: The Internet of Things

The biggest Internet trend for the 2010s was the **Internet of Things (IoT)** (see Chapter 6). The continued development of wireless technologies and sensors has enabled all kinds of devices to "talk" over the Internet. From wearables like the Apple Watch to smart TVs and connected cars, the 2010s heralded an age where almost any physical object can be part of the Internet.

What's more, the explosive growth in connected devices seems set to continue for some time. Gartner, a global research and advisory firm, estimated there were around 6.4 billion Internet-connected "things" in 2016. Other studies project this number to exceed 30 billion by 2025. With the mass deployment of the 5G mobile network (see Chapter 3) at the start of the 2020s, ubiquitous Internet access for everyone (and everything) is now the order of the day.

2

A Crash Course in Networking and Protocols

The ingenuity of the Internet is how it gives various devices and networks the ability to "talk" to one another. But what is the Internet? And how does it do what it does?

What is the Internet?

The **Internet** is an interconnected network of networks, connecting millions of computing devices around the world. Devices that connect to the Internet are often called **end systems** or **hosts**. This is because they operate at the "edge" of the network and host many of the individual Internet applications we use. A host may be running a number of **programs** (like a web browser) at any given time.

To communicate with other devices over the Internet, hosts slice up outgoing messages (made of bits—a one or a zero) into smaller data packets and send these packets into the "core" of the network. The network core consists of **packet switches**, which take incoming packets and forward them to their destination. Hosts and packet switches are connected by a range of physical media, which include copper wires, fiber-optic cables, and radio waves.

One of the principles behind the Internet's success is the idea of **pushing complexity to the edge of the network**. Hosts at the network edge handle computational tasks (such as running your favorite streaming app). This leaves the network core free to focus on delivering messages to where they need to go.

A flat view of the Internet

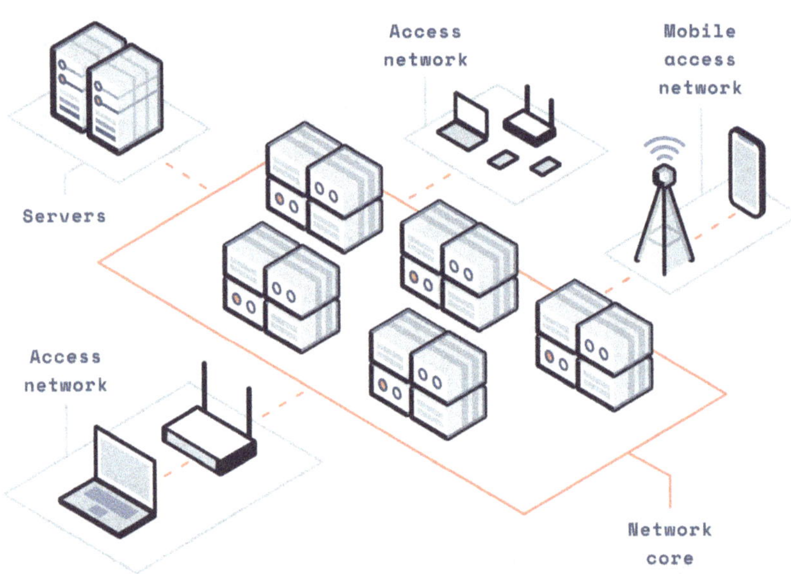

A rough picture of the Internet

The picture above gives a flat representation of the Internet. At the network edge, hosts connect to an **Internet access point** to form an **access network**. In a home setting, the Internet access point is a modem (although it's typically bundled with a router these days). If you're out and about, your mobile device will connect to a base station to form a mobile access network. An access network is connected to the wider Internet by a series of **routers** and **packet switches**. These routers and packet switches form the Internet's **network core.**

Modem vs. Switch vs. Router

There's often a lot of confusion about the differences between a modem, a router, and a switch. Here, we look at how these three devices are distinct. Don't worry if you don't understand some of the terms here. We'll get to them later in the chapter.

Modem: A modem brings the Internet to your home. It establishes a connection between your home network and your Internet service provider (ISP). Modems modulate digital computer signals into analog signals that can be sent over a phone line. It also performs the reverse operation: demodulating analog signals into digital signals. There are two main types of modems. Cable modems are connected via a coaxial cable to your cable provider. DSL (Digital Subscriber Line) modems are connected via your phone line.

Switch: A switch forwards packets to a device's physical address, also called a MAC address. Devices are typically connected to a switch via an Ethernet cable. Once a device is connected, the switch stores the MAC addresses of the device in a switch table so it knows which ports to send data to. Switches are the basis of local networks.

Router: A router "routes" packets to other devices using IP addresses. Once the destination for a packet is known, a router pushes that packet to its next stop (which can be another router) on the way to the destination. In a home setting, routers are used to route data to the devices in your home network. Most modern routers have built-in switches and accept wireless and Ethernet connections. While switches are used to create local networks, routers are used to connect networks.

Requests are sent from a client (e.g., a web browser) to a server. The server processes the request before sending the requested information back to the client. Whenever a request or response (made up of individual data packets) arrives at a router, the router clones the packets and sends them on to the next step of their journey, which may be another router or the intended destination.

In reality, the Internet is not simply a flat network as shown. Rather, it is made up of layers that each perform a function. A layered architecture is useful because it gives us a structured way to understand each component. It also allows changes to be made to one layer without drastically affecting the others. This "separation of concerns" is a principle that appears in other areas of computing and development. For example, in client-side web development, HTML is used to structure content. Other languages are responsible for styling (CSS) as well as logic and interactivity (JavaScript). By keeping these functions separate, developers can make changes to one aspect of the system without changing everything else.

One of the disadvantages of layering is that functionality may be duplicated across layers. Another issue is that information needed at one layer may be kept at a different layer. Despite these drawbacks, the rapid growth and scalability of the modern Internet is due in no small part to its layered architecture. The name given to the various layers of the Internet is the **protocol stack.**

The protocol stack

Before we introduce the various layers of the protocol stack, we need to understand why there is a need for all these protocols. Think about how you talk on the phone. The person receiving the call will typically speak first, both sides will confirm if now's a good time to talk, and both sides will acknowledge whether they've heard or failed to hear what the other person just said. In other words, we follow *protocols* in our communications.

Internet hosts behave in a similar way. They follow protocols that define how they should prepare messages, how messages will be sent, and what to do when a message is received. With protocols, developers don't have to worry about their application not playing nice with others. As long as the application follows the established rules, it will be able to prepare messages, send and receive them, and ultimately reassemble packets into meaningful messages.

The Internet protocol stack has five layers. It is a "condensed" version of the earlier seven-layer OSI (Open Systems Interconnection) reference model. Information travels down from the top layer to the bottom before entering the network. Once it reaches its destination, the information is reassembled and travels from the bottom layer to the top, where it is processed by the appropriate application.

The TCP/IP protocol stack

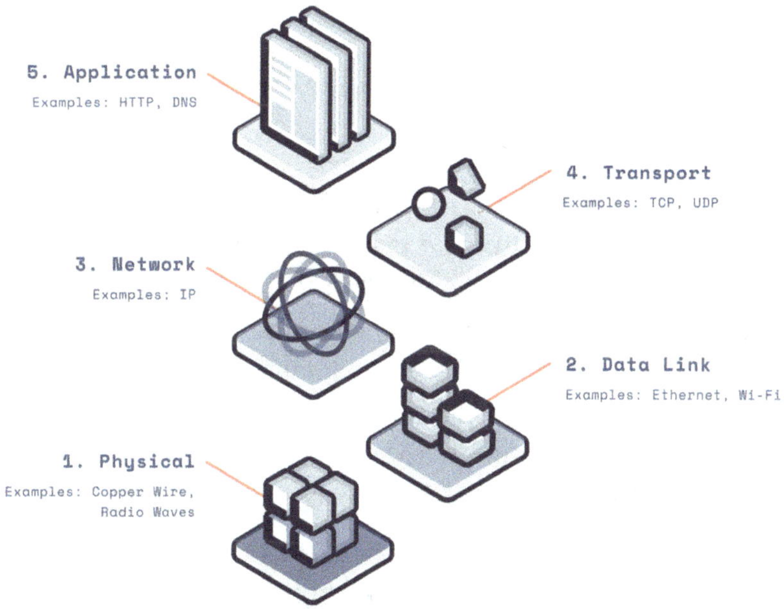

The application layer

The application layer contains the network applications we use as well as various **application-layer protocols**. These protocols define how messages are passed between processes. It defines what types of application messages are allowed, the rules for sending messages, and how to respond to a message when one arrives.

Here are some of the most important application-layer protocols.

HTTP

The Web, one of the most well-known Internet applications, uses **HTTP (Hypertext Transfer Protocol)** as its application-layer protocol. HTTP governs the communications between web clients (e.g., Mozilla Firefox) and web servers, ensuring requests and responses are made according to a common standard. By following HTTP, web clients make requests in a way that can be understood by servers, prompting the servers to return requested web pages or files.

DNS

Although not actually a protocol, the **DNS (Domain Name System)** is a vital Internet function and is located at the application layer. It acts as the Internet's phonebook, translating natural-language hostnames (e.g., www.google.com) into numeric IP addresses (e.g., 66.102.10.255). When you enter a hostname for the first time, your DNS client sends it to your ISP's DNS servers (unless you've configured your device to use another DNS server). At the end of the DNS query process, the DNS client receives a reply containing the IP address mapped to that hostname.

Depending on the top-level domain (TLD) you entered (e.g., .com, .net, .org, etc.), the DNS client will receive the IP address of an appropriate top-level domain server. These TLD servers store the addresses of various authoritative DNS servers, which contain the specific IP address for the hostname you entered. Once your DNS client returns the hostname, your device can request the resource belonging to that hostname.

A primer on DNS requests

This image shows a series of **iterative DNS queries**. Here, the local DNS server contacts the different "levels" of DNS servers individually to get the resource it needs.

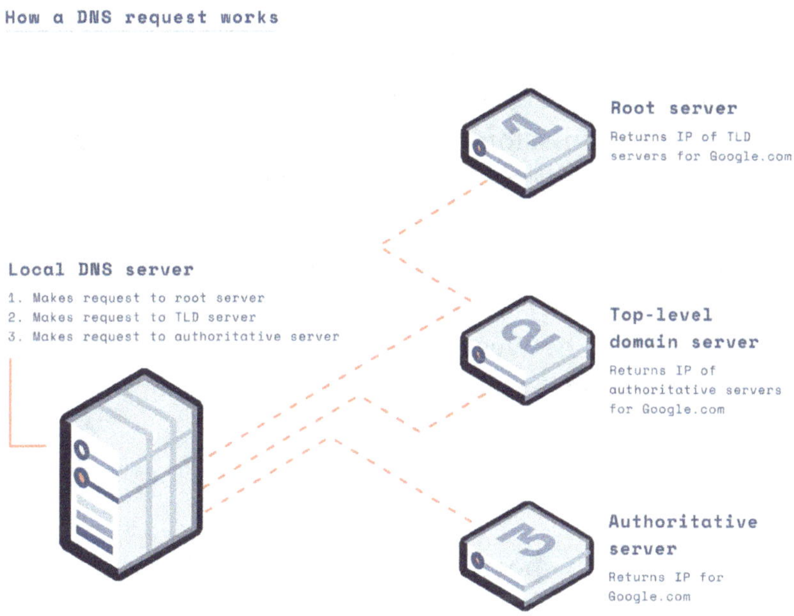

In **recursive DNS queries,** the contacted server helps the requesting server "ask" for the next piece of information needed. This means the requesting server does not have to wait for a reply from a contacted server before reaching out to another.

> In practice, queries between the host to the local DNS server are recursive, so the local DNS server does most of the "asking." By that logic, requests originating from the local DNS server are iterative.

Besides HTTP, other popular application-layer protocols include FTP (File Transfer Protocol) for transmitting files and SMTP (Simple Mail Transfer Protocol) for sending and receiving emails.

The transport layer

The transport layer takes application-layer messages and "transports" them between application endpoints. It is responsible for end-to-end transmission between processes, creating what is often called "logical communication" between processes. Logical communication between processes describes a situation where two application processes (e.g., two email programs) appear to be "talking" to each other directly, when in fact there is a long chain of intermediaries between them. This communication is made possible by **transport-layer protocols** that define how data is sent from one host to another.

TCP

Of the various transport-layer protocols, **TCP (Transmission Control Protocol)** and its younger sibling, **UDP (User Datagram Protocol)**, have remained most popular. At heart, both TCP and UDP provide process-to-process delivery. But as the more responsible older sibling, TCP will also check for delivery errors and retransmit lost packets. TCP also lowers transmission rates when the network is busy—a conscientious feature that has no doubt annoyed users from time to time!

To understand how TCP is able to resend lost communications, we need to look at the TCP "three-way handshake."

The TCP three-way handshake

In computer networking parlance, TCP is known as a connection-oriented protocol. This is because it requires the communicating processes on two hosts to establish a logical connection before data can be transferred. Under TCP, hosts go through a **three-way handshake** prior to data transfer. This is the process that opens a formal communication session between two hosts.

First, the TCP client sends a SYN (for "synchronize") segment and a sequence number to the server. This is a connection request from the client.

After the server has received the SYN segment, it returns a SYN-ACK segment and its own sequence number. This is a connection-granting acknowledgment that contains the variables to be used in the connection.

Finally, the client sends an ACK (for "acknowledgment") segment to the server. The hosts are now ready to communicate and transfer data.

The TCP three-way handshake

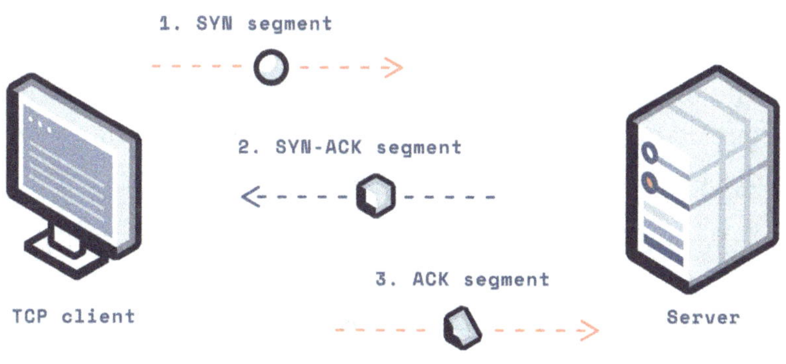

TCP uses a timer and sequence numbers to determine whether a packet needs to be retransmitted. If a segment has not been received past a set timeout interval, the sender will retransmit the segment. If the sequence number of a received segment indicates a prior segment was lost, the lost segment will be sent again. Lastly, if a segment is received with bit errors, it will be retransmitted as well.

UDP

Under UDP, applications simply pump out messages at a constant pace. This happens even if a portion of traffic is lost during transmission. Also, unlike TCP, UDP does not throttle its own traffic. This can lead to situations where UDP traffic "crowds out" TCP traffic in congested networks.

Video-conferencing applications typically run over UDP or will at least try UDP first. This means participants can have a real-time conversation even if a frame is dropped here and there. By contrast, high-definition streaming typically uses TCP. This is because the objective is to receive high-quality video and audio output—at the cost of occasional buffering when the network is busy.

The network layer

While the transport layer is responsible for message transmission, the network layer determines how packets reach their destination. The network layer houses the vital function of addressing and routing packets from one host to another. In other words, it provides logical communication between hosts.

Unlike the application and transport layers, which are only implemented in software, the network layer is implemented in both software and hardware. The "software side" is called the **control plane**. Here, a network-wide logic determines how packets are routed across routers to their destination. The "hardware side" is the **data plane**. The key activities on the data plane are performed on each router and govern how a packet arriving at a router's input links moves to that router's output links.

BGP

A group of routers under common administrative control is called an **Autonomous System (AS)**. An ISP may have one or more ASs in its infrastructure. For packets to travel across Autonomous Systems owned by different ISPs, the ASs follow the **Border Gateway Protocol (BGP)**. Arguably the "glue" of the Internet, BGP is the protocol that connects ISPs and, in effect, enables packets from one corner of the globe to be sent to another.

Each BGP-compliant router within an AS has a routing table that determines the shortest route to the destination network. Routing rules and tables are manually configured, and can be updated as needed. BGP routers also continually exchange route information. This keeps the Internet updated with the latest routing rules.

While BGP takes care of routing between Autonomous Systems, routing *within* an AS is controlled by intra-AS routing protocols such as **Open Shortest Path First (OSPF)**.

IP

While BGP connects Autonomous Systems into the network of networks we call the Internet, the **Internet Protocol (IP)** provides the addressing format used by every Internet-connected host. There are two versions of IP in use today—**IPv4** and **IPv6**.

IPv4 uses 32-bit addresses and has been in use since 1983. An example of an IPv4 address is 172.16.254.10.

In the '90s, the Internet Engineering Task Force began to work on a long-term successor to IPv4. The result, IPv6, was introduced in

2012. Using 128-bit addresses, IPv6 provides significantly more available addresses and also includes security improvements over its predecessor. The huge increase in available IP addresses is important in areas like the Internet of Things (see Chapter 6), where a multitude of individual devices are connected and sending data to one another. An example of an IPv6 address is 2001:0db8:85a3:0000:0000:8a2e:0370:7334.

DHCP

When a host connects to the Internet, it receives an IP address by following the **Dynamic Host Configuration Protocol (DHCP)**. The host broadcasts a "DHCP discovery" message that is picked up by a DHCP server. The DHCP server forms a "DHCP offer" message, containing a proposed IP address and other session parameters, and sends it back to the host.

If the host accepts the offer, it broadcasts a formal request for that IP address and waits for confirmation from the server. This might seem redundant, but it is needed for handling cases where there is more than one DHCP server on the network offering IP addresses. Once the DHCP server has acknowledged the request, the host "owns" the IP address for a set duration.

The DHCP process

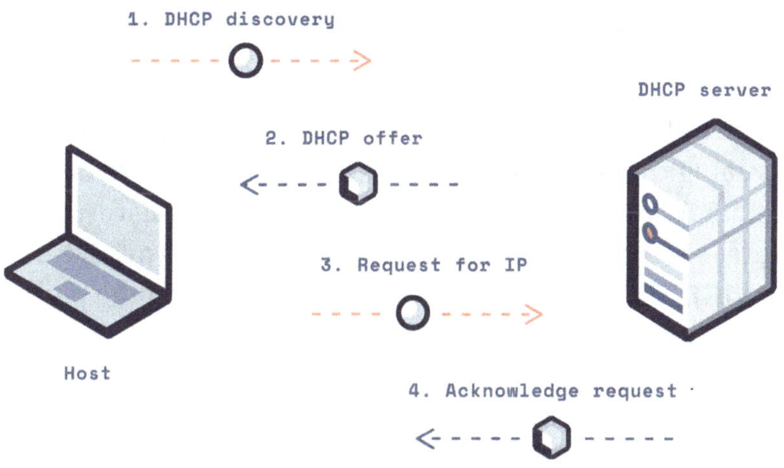

Having looked at DNS (at the application layer), IP addresses, and BGP, we have now met the three core components that enable packets to be sent across the Internet.

DNS	Function: **Naming**
The DNS translates a human-readable hostname to an IP address that servers can understand.	
IP address	Function: **Addressing**
The IP address reveals a host's "location" on the Internet. IP addresses are often assigned by DHCP.	
BGP	Function: **Routing**
BGP is used to determine the path a packet should travel to its destination. Autonomous Systems owned by different ISPs follow BGP to exchange routing information. While a packet is moving within an AS, it follows an intra-AS routing protocol like OSPF.	

The data link layer

So far, we've dealt with how messages are prepared and transported, as well as how they find their way across the Internet. That leaves one crucial question: How do packets actually move across the network?

The answer lies in the data link layer, where data packets (often called datagrams) are physically moved from one network node to another. While the link layer is a combination of hardware and software, it is mostly implemented in a device's **network interface card (NIC)**. The network interface card (also called the network adapter) is the hardware component that actually connects a computer to a network.

LANs, WANs, and MAC addresses

Before the emergence of the Internet, devices were connected in **local area networks (LANs)**. For example, a group of office computers connected to each other by coaxial cable would form a LAN. Each of these computers (or more accurately, the network adapter within each computer) will have a **MAC address** (media access control address). This gives the computers a way to "talk" to their peers on the LAN, but they wouldn't be able to communicate with a group of computers on the other side of the globe. At least until the emergence of IP addresses.

Nowadays, every Internet-connected device has at least one IP address and a MAC address. This may seem redundant and confusing at first. Why do we need both IP addresses (at the network layer) and MAC addresses (at the data link layer)?

First, let's look at the differences between the two. MAC addresses are globally unique. The Institute of Electrical and Electronics Engineers (IEEE) manages and sells portions of the available MAC address space to manufacturers worldwide. The manufacturers then assign a unique MAC address to each network adapter. IP addresses, on the other hand, are assigned to a host when they connect to the Internet and can change as the host moves. For example, a laptop may be assigned a certain IP address when it's on the first floor of an office building but can be given another when carried to the second floor.

More importantly, a host may have a number of IP addresses, but it will have only one MAC address (if it has only one network interface card). This happens when the host is connected to several different networks at the same time. In these situations, the host will have an IP address for each network connection.

The need for MAC addresses becomes clear when numerous LANs join together to form **wide area networks (WANs)**. IP addresses are used on the Internet to refer to a specific host and the LAN it "lives" in. But once a message arrives in a LAN, it is delivered to the MAC address unique to the host's network interface card. Think of an IP address as a postal address and the MAC address as your full name. Your postal address tells the mail service where to deliver a letter meant for you. But once the letter arrives in your mailbox, your name tells you (and anybody else sharing your mailbox) that you are the intended recipient of the letter.

ARP

The need to translate between IP addresses and MAC addresses led to the creation of the **Address Resolution Protocol (ARP)**. Each host and router contains an ARP table that maps IP addresses to MAC addresses. If the sender's ARP table doesn't contain the MAC address of the recipient, the sender broadcasts an ARP packet to query the other hosts and routers on the subnet. Once an answer is received, the sending host can update its own ARP table to handle future IP-MAC translations.

Ethernet, Wi-Fi, and Bluetooth

We can't end our discussion of LANs and the data link layer without discussing **Ethernet**. Since its introduction in 1973, Ethernet has quickly become the dominant wired LAN technology. It was the first widely deployed high-speed LAN technology and continually evolved to keep pace with changing standards. Most importantly, Ethernet was cheaper and simpler compared with rivals like Token Ring, which helped it achieve mass adoption. Today, the numerous Ethernet standards are maintained by the IEEE 802.3 working group.

Of the many different Ethernet standards, **Wi-Fi** is likely the most well-known. Following the IEEE's standard for wireless LANs (IEEE 802.11), Wi-Fi operates by sending radio signals at specific frequency ranges (typically between 2.4–2.485 GHz and 5.1–5.875 GHz). To use Wi-Fi, a device's wireless adapter connects to a wireless access point using radio signals. The wireless access point then connects the device to the Internet via a variety of methods, including land-based broadband connections or a satellite link.

A similar technology is **Bluetooth**. Unlike Wi-Fi, which is designed for wireless LANs and Internet connectivity, Bluetooth was created for mobile devices to communicate over very short distances. Using ultra high frequency radio waves, Bluetooth offers roughly one-tenth of the range available to Wi-Fi and cannot support as many users. On the flip side, it also consumes less power than Wi-Fi.

We will look at Wi-Fi and Bluetooth in more detail in the next chapter.

The physical layer

The physical layer is the actual infrastructure on which data is transferred. It consists of hardware (unless the network is virtualized, i.e., simulated by software) and its main function is to transmit bits between devices.

Bits are transmitted via links, which may be copper wires, fiber-optic cable, or radio waves.

The basics of connecting to the Internet and a web request

Now that we understand each layer of the protocol stack, let's put the pieces together and look at a basic web request. For this example, let's assume we're accessing www.google.com on a laptop that's connected to a router via an Ethernet cable.

Connecting to an access network

The first step is to connect your laptop to an access network. Remember that the Internet is a network of networks, so you're not actually connecting to some abstract entity called "the Internet." Instead, you connect your laptop to an access network (such as your home Wi-Fi network) that is connected to your ISP's network. Your ISP's network is connected to networks owned by other ISPs. These networks, in turn, connect the server or host you're trying to reach.

Connecting to your ISP's network (and beyond)

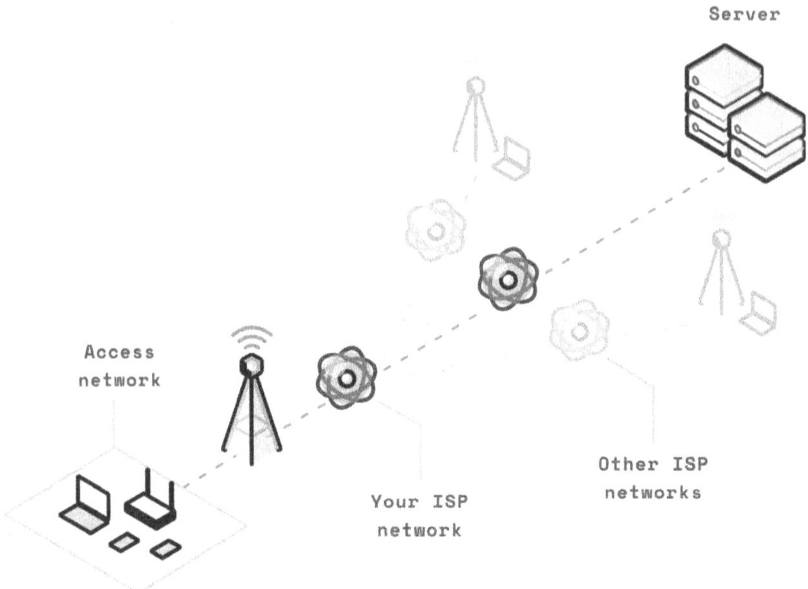

If you're indoors, your access network is likely your home, school, or office LAN. Devices in a LAN are often connected to an edge router by Ethernet cable or by Wi-Fi. If you're out and about, you'll likely be using wireless cellular data (see Chapter 3). In this example, our laptop is connected to the access network via an Ethernet cable.

Getting an IP address: DHCP

After your laptop is connected to your home router (via an Ethernet cable), it needs to get an IP address. The IP address acts as an identifier for your laptop, so other devices know where to send messages intended for you. To do this, your laptop broadcasts a DHCP request message to every other host on the LAN. The DHCP server in your router receives this message and sends a DHCP offer message containing a proposed IP address and a few other parameters.

When your laptop receives the DHCP offer, it broadcasts a request to use the proposed IP address. Once the DHCP server acknowledges the request, your cable-connected laptop officially has an IP address it can use to access the Internet. It also knows the address of the DNS server it will use and where to send any traffic external to its LAN.

Finding the IP of the resource: DNS (and ARP, OSPF, and BGP)

To visit Google, your web browser has to request an IP address that's mapped to "www.google.com." Let's assume neither your browser nor router has any of these IP addresses cached (i.e., saved) in memory. To find the IP address, your laptop creates a DNS query message intended for its assigned DNS server.

When your laptop sends the DNS query to the DNS server, the packets must first pass through your gateway router. Your laptop knows the gateway router's IP address but does not know its MAC address. To find the MAC address mapped to the gateway router's IP address, your laptop uses ARP.

Once the DNS query has passed through the gateway router, the packets need to find a way to the DNS server. Here, routing protocols like OSPF (for routing within an ISP's network) and BGP (for routing between networks owned by different ISPs) are used to determine the best path for your query.

Once the DNS query reaches the DNS server, the server will find a valid IP address mapped to "www.google.com." There are two ways to achieve this: Either the DNS server has a cached copy of the address, or it'll ask another server for the address it needs. Once the DNS server has found the IP address, it will send a DNS reply message, containing the IP address mapped to "www.google.com," back to your laptop.

Your browser and router will temporarily store this mapping in their respective memories of recent DNS lookups. This is so they don't have to ask a DNS server for an IP address each time you visit Google. It also reduces the number of DNS messages sent across the Internet and lowers the chances of attacks like DNS poisoning (see Chapter 4). However, because hostname-IP mappings change over time, DNS caches periodically discard saved entries to make way for new mappings.

Connecting to the resource: TCP

Your web browser now knows which IP address to request. Since the Web uses TCP as its transport-layer protocol, the next step is for your web browser to establish a connection with Google's web server. This is done via a three-way handshake (see page 23) that indicates both sides are ready and available to communicate.

Your browser begins the handshake process by sending a TCP SYN segment to the server. The server acknowledges receipt by returning a TCP SYN-ACK segment. Your browser sends an ACK segment to the server (to acknowledge the server's acknowledgment). This completes the TCP three-way handshake and creates a TCP socket. A socket is simply an endpoint for sending and receiving data.

Requesting the resource: HTTP

With the TCP connection established, your browser can now request the desired content from Google's server. This is done by sending an HTTP request into the TCP socket. When the server receives the request, it forms an HTTP response (containing the requested web page) and sends the response into the TCP socket. Once the HTTP response message reaches your web browser, your browser extracts the page from the response and displays it. Voilà!

At the end of the communication session, your browser sends a FIN segment to the server and receives an ACK segment in return. The session is terminated after the server sends its own FIN segment to your browser and receives a corresponding ACK segment. (In practice, TCP allows either party to initiate closing the connection.)

And that, in a nutshell, is how a host connects to the Internet and sends web requests. It may seem simple from the comfort of your chair, but there's a lot that goes on for a web page to reach you!

3

Going Mobile

In the previous chapter, we looked at Internet access on a fixed, stationary host. That picture was all you needed to know prior to 1991, when mobile Internet access first became possible.

In this chapter, we'll examine the evolution of mobile networks and the challenges that come with mobile users accessing the Internet via wireless hosts.

Wireless vs. mobile Internet access

First, let's draw a distinction between wireless and mobile Internet access. The two terms are often used interchangeably but do not mean the same thing.

A **wireless** host is connected to a network using a wireless communication standard (such as Wi-Fi) but may not always be mobile. If you're sitting at your desk and working on your laptop over Wi-Fi, you're using a form of (nonmobile) wireless Internet access.

A **mobile** host is one that has different network attachment points over time and may even transition between different access networks. If you're streaming a show on your phone while riding a bus, you're accessing the Internet via a mobile host.

Below, we'll look at some of the most common wireless technology standards like Wi-Fi, Bluetooth, and mobile data networks.

Wireless local area networks: Wi-Fi

Wi-Fi is perhaps the most well-known area network technology. As a member of the IEEE 802.11 family of standards, Wi-Fi is the standard's definition for wireless LANs.

Under the Wi-Fi standard, wireless hosts connect to an **access point (AP)**. Multiple APs are typically serviced by a switch or router. In home settings, the access point and router are usually bundled into one device.

Access points make themselves known to hosts by periodically broadcasting **beacon frames**. To connect to an access point, a user selects the AP's **service set identifier (SSID)**, colloquially called "the Wi-Fi name." An SSID is usually protected by a password. Once connected, the user's device is associated with that AP and will only receive packets from that AP (even if there are other accessible APs in the area). Because Wi-Fi operates at the 2.4 GHz and 5 GHz frequency bands, most APs will have two SSIDs—one for each frequency band.

Speeds for Wi-Fi vary. The latest iteration of Wi-Fi, 802.11ax (a.k.a. Wi-Fi 6), is capable of maximum speeds of 9.6 Gbps. This is a significant improvement over 802.11ac (Wi-Fi 5), which topped out at around 3.5 Gbps. Wi-Fi 6 achieves these higher speeds via better data encoding, leading to a signal that's packed with more data. Beyond faster speeds, Wi-Fi 6 also creates less overhead and latency than its predecessors. This is done via a new method for multiplexing (defined in the section on 2G), called **orthogonal frequency-division multiple access (OFDMA)**. Altogether, these improvements allow Wi-Fi 6 to offer greater network stability and reliability when servicing large groups of devices.

Wireless personal area networks: Bluetooth

While Wi-Fi is intended to work over a distance of around 300 feet (roughly 100 meters), there are networking technologies that are intended for use in smaller areas. These technologies give rise to what are often called **wireless personal area networks (WPANs)**. The most popular WPAN technology is Bluetooth, often used for devices like wireless keyboards and earphones.

Bluetooth follows the IEEE 802.15.1 standard and has an effective range of around 30 feet. It was designed as a type of low-power, short-range connective technology and is often used to connect Internet of Things (IoT) devices (see Chapter 6). Unlike Wi-Fi, which operates in both the 2.4 GHz and 5 GHz bands, Bluetooth operates at the 2.4 GHz band.

Bluetooth also does not carry the same network infrastructure requirements as Wi-Fi. While Wi-Fi hosts need to connect to access points, Bluetooth hosts self-organize into a **piconet**. The host that initiates the piconet and controls communications is the **master**. All other devices are **slaves** that can only transmit to the master. Piconets are formed differently based on whether Bluetooth is being used in Basic Rate/Enhanced Data Rate (BR/EDR) mode or Low Energy (LE) mode.

Besides Bluetooth, Zigbee is another frequently used WPAN technology. Based on the IEEE 802.15.4 standard, Zigbee also works in the 2.4 GHz spectrum but is designed to consume even less power than Bluetooth. Many IoT devices use Zigbee as the protocol of choice.

The evolution of mobile networks

Wi-Fi lets us enjoy the Internet wirelessly, but true mobile Internet access comes from advancements in cellular communications. Here, we summarize the history of mobile networks, from the first generation of mobile standards to 5G.

1G

The first generation of wireless cellular technology (1G) was introduced in the 1980s and saw service until the early '90s.

1G handsets were bulky, communicated on the analog public telephone network, and only supported voice transmissions. Data transmission rates topped out at around 2.4 Kbps. To put that in perspective, if you were to download a full season of *The Simpsons* (around 1.8 GB) at that speed, you'd have to wait for almost 75 days for the download to finish. D'oh!

2G

In the late '90s, the world transitioned to 2G. Like its predecessor, 2G used the public switched telephone network as its core network and did not support the Internet. That said, 2G featured improved speeds (up to around 10 Kbps) and, despite starting life as a voice-only network, was later "upgraded" to support basic data transfer. Dubbed "2.5G," this expanded version of 2G increased data transmission rates to around 64 Kbps.

2G was also significant for introducing different standards for converting data into radio waves. The two largest camps are **GSM** (used in Europe and Asia) and **CDMA** (used mostly in the U.S.). Although both systems used similar cellular architectures, GSM and CDMA differed in their approaches to **SIM (subscriber identification module)** cards and to multiplexing (the act of sending multiple signal strands over a shared medium).

GSM vs. CDMA: SIM cards

Hosts in a GSM network use SIM cards. Each SIM card contains subscriber information (such as your service subscription and address book) and is required for a subscriber to connect to the mobile network. If you are replacing your phone, you can simply insert your existing SIM card into the new phone and continue using your current subscription.

In CDMA networks, hosts do not use SIM cards. This is because each phone has an embedded serial number and is built specifically to work on one carrier network. Before 4G LTE phones, if you decided to change carriers, you would also need to switch phones.

GSM vs. CDMA: Multiplexing

Multiplexing is about combining multiple signals into one signal over a common medium. In other words, multiplexing is the technology that allows numerous mobile users to communicate over the same cellular infrastructure at the same time.

GSM (Global System for Mobile Communications) networks use a channel access method called **time-division multiple access (TDMA)**. With TDMA, all of the available channel bandwidth is made available to a user for a period of time before rotating to the next user for the next period. For example, if two users are using a TDMA channel, each user may have access to the full channel for 50 milliseconds before the channel is "allocated" to the other user. This quick back-and-forth switching gives each user the impression they are the sole user of the channel.

CDMA networks use **code-division multiple access**. Unlike TDMA, there is no time-based rotation of channel availability. Instead, all bandwidth is made available to all users, who are separated and identified by a unique CDMA code.

2G cellular network architecture

The 2G mobile network

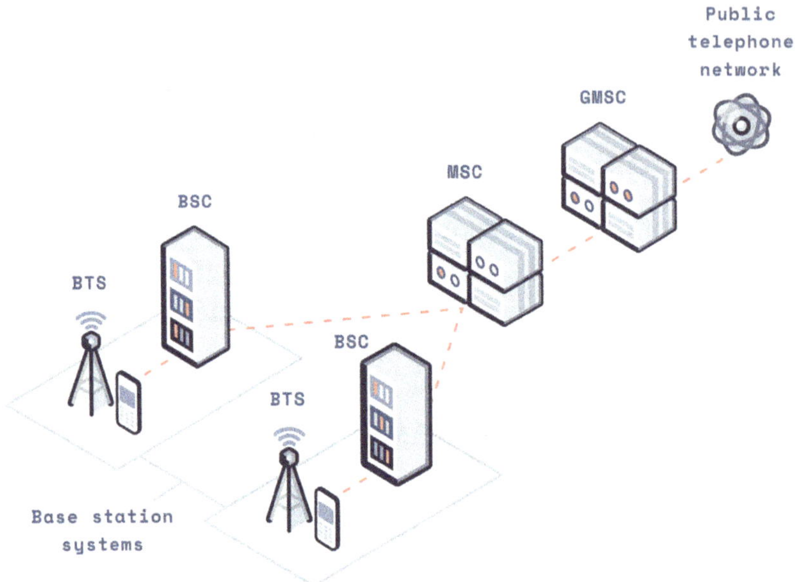

In a 2G network, mobile hosts connect to a **base transceiver station (BTS)**. Each BTS (or base station) serves hosts in its designated area or "cell" (leading to the term "cell phone"). Multiple BTSs are controlled by a **base station controller (BSC)**, whose job is to allocate BTS radio channels, identify mobile users in a cell, and perform mobile handoffs. Finally, multiple BSCs are serviced by a **mobile switching center (MSC)**, which is connected to a **gateway mobile switching center (GMSC)**. The gateway MSC is connected to the public telephone network.

3G

3G was commercially launched in 2001 and moved to a packet-switched network supporting the TCP/IP protocol stack. Data transmission rates increased to around 2 Mbps and could now support voice, data, and images. In many ways, 3G marked the beginning of mobile Internet usage as we know it today.

Like 2G, 3G featured different mobile standards. The **UMTS (Universal Mobile Telecommunications Service)** standard was introduced as a result of work on GSM while CDMA was succeeded by **CDMA2000**.

3G network architecture (UMTS)

The 3G mobile network (UMTS)

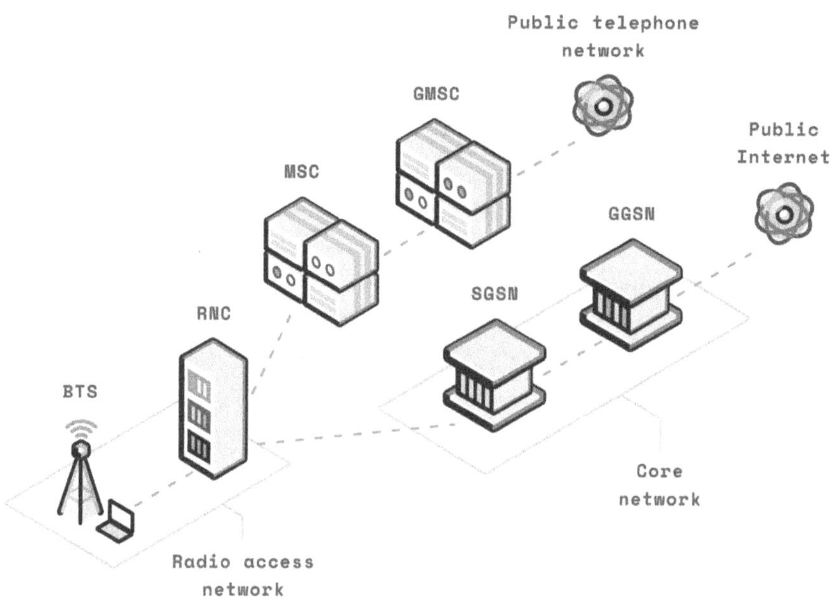

Under UMTS, mobile hosts can connect to the Internet in addition to accessing the public telephone network, as they did under the 2G GSM standard. When connecting to the public telephone network, hosts first connect to a **radio network controller (RNC)** to join a **radio access network (RAN)**. The RNC then connects to an MSC and GMSC before reaching the public telephone network.

To link a device to the Internet, the RNC first connects to a **serving GPRS support node (SGSN)**. The SGSN is responsible for delivering packets to and from mobile devices in its radio access network. The

SGSN then connects to a **gateway GPRS support node (GGSN)**, which services multiple SGSNs and is the last stop before a UMTS device connects to the Internet. These two components form the 3G core network under UMTS.

3G network architecture (CDMA2000)

The 3G mobile network (CDMA2000)

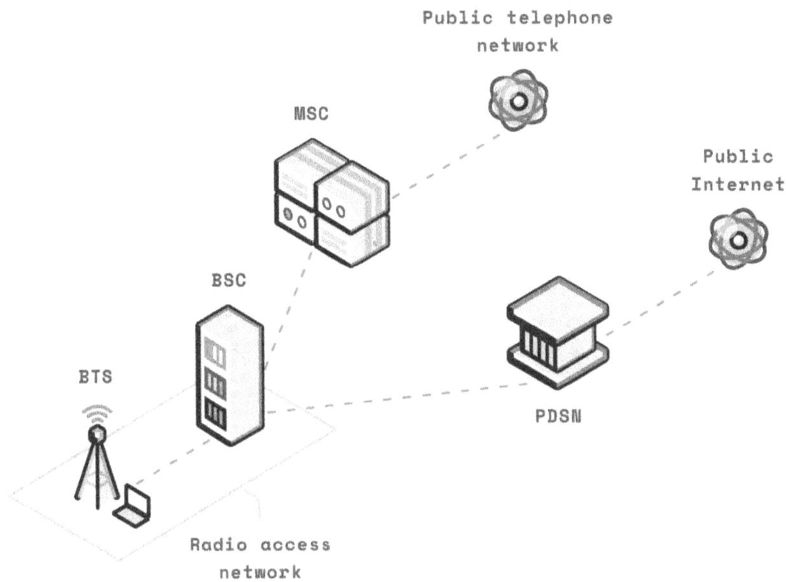

As with UMTS, CDMA2000 doesn't change the way a mobile device connects to the public telephone network. When connecting to the Internet, a device will still link to a base station but will then reach a **packet data serving node (PDSN)**. This component is unique to the CDMA2000 architecture, functioning as a bridge between the radio access network and packet data networks like the Internet.

4G

Launched in 2009, 4G represented a move toward unifying the standards used by mobile devices. 4G's **LTE (Long-Term Evolution)** standard introduced an enhanced radio access network and can be used by both CDMA and GSM networks.

A second innovation that came with 4G was an all-IP core network, often called the Evolved Packet Core (EPC). With its all-IP core network, 4G can handle data transmissions of around 100 Mbps and does not require separate networks for voice and data. With 4G, both voice and data are carried in IP packets.

4G network architecture

The 4G mobile network

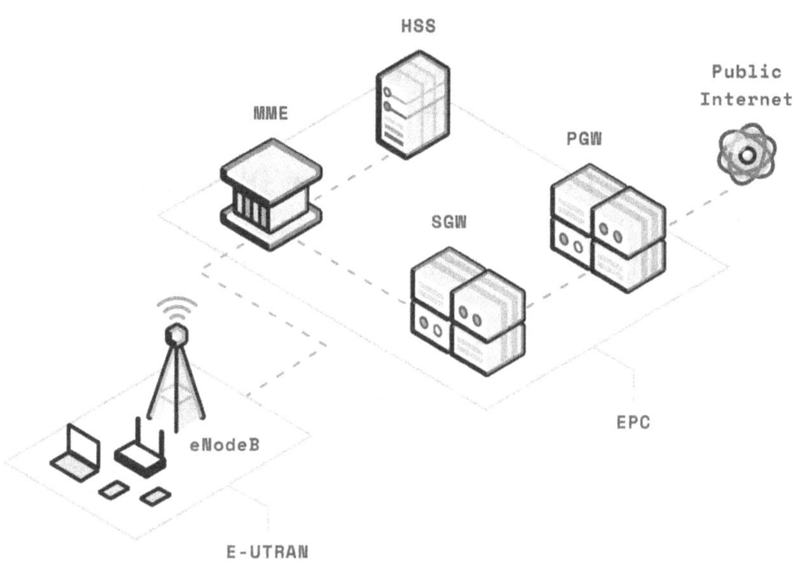

The 4G network can be broken down into two neat parts: the **Evolved Universal Terrestrial Radio Access Network (E-UTRAN)** and the **Evolved Packet Core (EPC)**.

In the E-UTRAN, the **user equipment** (4G-speak for a mobile host) connects to an **eNodeB (Evolved Node B)**. The eNodeB replaces the 2G base station and the 3G radio network controller, performing the vital job of connecting the user equipment to the EPC. Besides this core task, the eNodeB also allocates channel resources, performs handovers, and handles transmission and congestion control when needed.

The Evolved Packet Core has four major components.

1. The **Mobility Management Entity (MME)** is the key control node and is responsible for authenticating the user, security, and location tracking.

2. The **Home Subscriber Server (HSS)** provides subscriber information to the MME and also houses information like maximum data rates and quality of service profiles.

3. The **Serving Gateway (SGW)** forwards all traffic between the user equipment and the Packet Data Network Gateway. It also performs billing functions.

4. The **Packet Data Network Gateway (PGW)** is the endpoint of the Evolved Packet Core. It allocates IP addresses to the user equipment and connects serviced users to the Internet.

5G

As of this writing, the world is acclimating to the deployment of 5G. Launched commercially at the end of 2020, 5G uses higher frequencies to deliver speeds up to 10 Gbps. Perhaps the biggest point of departure between 5G and its predecessors is that the 5G network architecture is software- and cloud-based. We'll soon see why this distinction is important.

5G system architecture consists of a **Core Network (CN)** and **next-generation radio access networks (NG-RAN).** Connection between the CN and a NG-RAN is made possible by a range of

transport network technologies. Examples of these transport network technologies include advanced optical network solutions, Ethernet, Space Division Multiplexing, and satellite systems.

Below, we go into more detail about the two main parts of the 5G system architecture.

The 5G mobile network

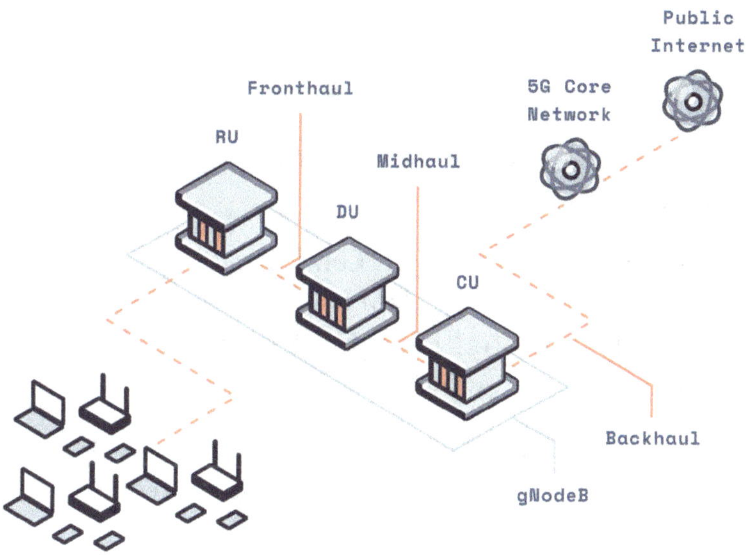

5G Core Network

The 5G Core Network is composed of **service-based architecture (SBA)** components. In a service-based architecture, components of the system provide services to one another via a common communication protocol. This architecture was chosen for the 5G Core Network because 5G is designed to be a "universal" standard that enables a broad palette of technological and business applications. For this to work, the next-generation Core Network must make it possible for a wide range of components to "talk" and exchange services with one another.

Another important feature of the 5G Core Network is the separation of its control plane from the user plane. This separation allows the control plane to be implemented "centrally" while the user plane is deployed in multiple locations and, more importantly, closer to end users. The rationale behind this design is to make user plane deployment more "flexible"—to bring it closer to the applications that rely on it. Be it video streaming or connected cars, having the user plane close to end users brings benefits like reduced latency and less bandwidth consumed.

5G Next Generation Radio Access Network

Each 5G NG-RAN is a collection of **gNodeBs (gNB)**. Each gNB has three modules:

1. **Centralized Unit (CU)**: A Centralized Unit is responsible for functions like user data transfer, session management, and mobility control. Each gNodeB has one CU that controls numerous Distributed Units.

2. **Distributed Unit (DU)**: Each DU is responsible for a subset of the functions carried out by the controlling CU. The specific functions allocated to a DU is determined by the CU.

3. **Radio Unit (RU)**: Used in certain deployments to extend the coverage of the gNodeB.

5G deployment

Unlike its predecessors, 5G can be flexibly deployed in a few ways. The differences depend on how the following aspects of the mobile network are implemented:

- **Backhaul**: The connection between the gNB (i.e., the radio access network) and the 5G Core Network.

- **Midhaul**: The connection between the Centralized Unit and the Distributed Unit within the gNB.

- **Fronthaul**: The connection between the gNB (i.e., the radio access network) and the Radio Unit.

Initial 5G New Radio (NR) launches leveraged existing 4G LTE infrastructure, running 5G NR software on 4G LTE hardware. Once the technology matures, 5G will enter what's called "stand-alone" mode. This just means 5G New Radio software will operate on 5G NR radio hardware with the 5G Core Network.

Hardware is one of the biggest hurdles to widespread 5G deployment. The highest 5G speeds require very powerful and expensive transmitters. Naturally, it will take time for wireless carriers to roll out the infrastructure needed for a high-speed 5G network at scale.

Mobile IP

Let's put the pieces together. How does a mobile device get an IP address and what happens to that address when the device enters a different network? How does your device maintain Internet access?

First, we need to distinguish between a **home network** and a **foreign network**. As you may have guessed, the home network is the network a host usually "lives" in. A foreign network is any other network the host may join. If you go for a walk outside with your phone, it might connect to one foreign network when you're passing through a park and another while you're shopping at the supermarket.

Within a home network, there is a **home agent** (typically a router) that stores information (such as location and IP address) about connected devices. Similarly, mobility management in foreign networks is done by **foreign agents**.

When a mobile host is in its home network, packets are sent to and from its home address via the usual IP process. When the host leaves its home network, it needs to register with a foreign agent. The host can begin this process by responding to agent advertisement messages sent by available foreign agents or by broadcasting its own agent solicitation message.

Once the mobile host has selected and registered with a foreign agent, it receives a **care-of address (COA)**. The foreign agent will share the mobile host's COA with its home agent and alert the home agent that the host is now in its (foreign) network. Packets sent to the host's home address will be forwarded to its care-of address while the host is in the foreign network.

This method of directing packets to a host's care-of address is called **indirect routing**. To perform indirect routing of packets, the home agent encapsulates a packet (intended for the host's home address) in another packet that's addressed to the host's COA. If the mobile host moves from one foreign network to another, the same registration and COA assignment is done with the new foreign agent. During this time, the host may experience some packet loss.

4

Internet Security

The Internet was originally designed to be a shared resource between trusted users. But as the Internet opened up for public use in the '90s, it didn't take long for people to use it for malicious purposes.

Unlike system failures, which are often "internal" and can be solved with more reliable infrastructure, attacks on the Internet stem from bad actors preying on unsuspecting users or unprotected systems. This leads to the need for network security.

This chapter explores the basics of network security. We'll first look at the many aspects of security before moving on to cryptography. Finally, we'll explore common types of cyberattacks and how to defend against them.

The concepts explored in this chapter are important for any modern Internet user and will be fundamental to understanding the content of the next chapter, on blockchain.

Six aspects of security

When most people think about Internet security, they generally think about firewalls, viruses, and hackers. While these are important components in the field of security, they don't provide a definition for it.

Simply put, network security is the field concerned with protecting the confidentiality, integrity, and availability of networks. In addition to these three core properties, endpoint authentication, nonrepudiation of actions, and privacy are also highly valuable attributes.

Six aspects of security

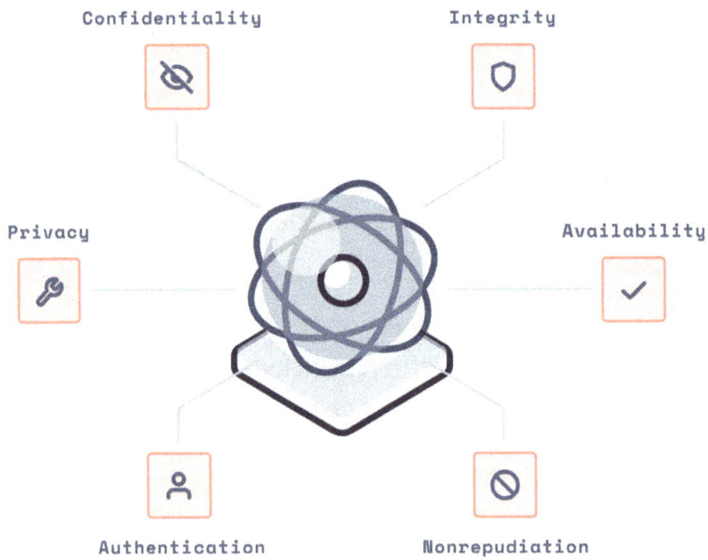

Confidentiality: Only the sender and intended recipient of a message should be able to access the contents of the message.

Integrity: Messages sent over the network are safe from intentional or accidental modification while in transit.

Availability: The network can continually function as intended.

Nonrepudiation: Users cannot deny actions conducted over the network.

(Endpoint) Authentication: Users can verify each other's identity.

Privacy: Users have control over their online information. This is often confused with anonymity, where users can hide their true identity. A museum's donor wall maintains privacy but not anonymity—it highlights the names of the donors without disclosing the amounts each donor gave. On the flip side, cryptocurrencies often focus on anonymity but not privacy—you might be able to transact without tying your account to your physical identity, but every transaction is recorded for all to see.

Cryptography and the basics of encryption

Cryptography is an essential part of computer and network security. Broadly defined, it is the field of disguising (or translating) messages so they are protected from unintended recipients.

In practice, cryptography involves taking **plaintext** and applying an **encryption key** to it. This produces **ciphertext**. Once the encrypted ciphertext is produced, it can be sent over an unsecure channel (like the Internet) to its intended recipient. To recover the plaintext, the recipient applies the correct **decryption key** to "reverse" the encryption.

How encryption and decryption work

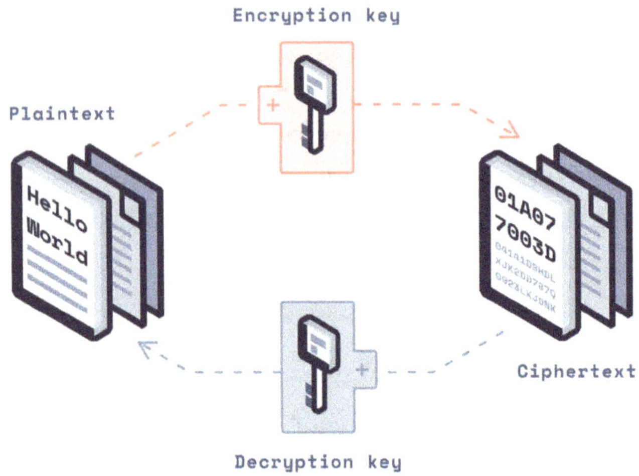

Encryption keys are generated by **encryption algorithms**. While encryption keys should be carefully protected, modern encryption algorithms are actually widely known. Public lockers make a useful analogy: Everyone knows the same type of lock (i.e., encryption algorithm) is used for each locker, but you can't open an individual locker if you don't know the number combination (i.e., the encryption/decryption key).

There are two main types of encryption:

In **symmetric key encryption**, the encryption and decryption keys are the same. Because there is only one key used in symmetric key cryptography, it must be kept secret at all times and is therefore called the **secret key**. DES (Data Encryption Standard) and AES (Advanced Encryption Standard) are symmetric key algorithms.

How symmetric key encryption works

In **public key encryption**, the encryption key can be made public. The decryption key is only known to the recipient. When using public key encryption, the sender encrypts the message with the recipient's public key before sending it. The recipient applies their private key to the ciphertext to decrypt the message. RSA (Rivest–Shamir–Adleman) is a well-known public key algorithm.

How public key encryption works

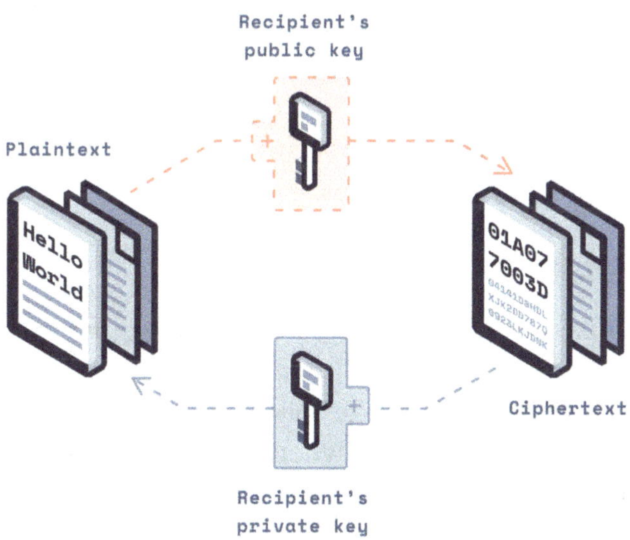

Before we move on to cryptographic applications, it's important to stress that encryption is not a silver bullet for every security problem. Encryption algorithms are very hard to break, but attackers have been able to crack poorly implemented encryption systems by looking at other vulnerabilities. During the Cold War, Soviet intelligence was able to decrypt over 3,000 messages from Western countries by simply reusing old keys. In effect, modern cryptography has transformed encryption problems into key-management problems.

Used properly, encryption keeps your data and files safe. But keep in mind it can also be used for nefarious purposes. Attackers can just as easily use encryption to stop you from accessing your files or devices. Locky (released in 2016) and WannaCry (2017) are two examples of ransomware used to encrypt a victim's files and extort payment.

Cryptographic applications for message integrity

In the previous section, we looked at the basics of cryptography and how encryption can keep messages safe from prying eyes, even when the messages are traveling over an unsecure medium like the Internet.

Now, we delve into another important use for cryptography: maintaining the integrity of messages.

Cryptographic hash functions

A **hash** is a fixed-length "fingerprint" of a message. For any message *m*, a hash algorithm can compute a unique hash ***h(m)***. Even the smallest changes to the message will produce a very different hash. This makes hashes very useful when checking whether a message has been modified or tampered with.

Unlike encryption, which is a "two-way" cryptographic process, hashing is a one-way operation: It is impossible to reverse-engineer a hashed value to reveal the original message. This is because the set of all possible messages (including messages of any length) is so much bigger than the set of fixed-length, hashed messages. It's therefore impossible to come up with a function that "reverses" hashes to give the original input.

A well-known hashing algorithm is SHA-256. With SHA-256, the output is always 256 bits (or 32 bytes) in length.

Message authentication codes

A hash can ensure a message isn't tampered with or modified, but it cannot guarantee that a particular message is what the original sender intended to send. This is where **message authentication codes (MAC)** come into play.

To use a MAC, two communicating parties need a shared secret key, *k*. The sender generates the MAC by calculating the hash of the message and the key, *h(m+k)*. The original message and the MAC, *m* and *h(m+k)*, are sent to the recipient.

When the recipient receives *m* and *h(m+k)*, they can use *k* and *m* to calculate *h(m+k)*. If the calculated hash is equal to the MAC, the recipient can be sure the message was sent by the real sender (assuming they are the only ones who know the secret key).

Digital signature

As the name suggests, **digital signatures** can be used to verify the identity of a person online. Unlike hashes and MACs, digital signatures use public key encryption to prove, in an unforgeable way, that someone is who they claim to be.

To digitally sign a document, the signer produces a hash of the document and applies their private key to it. To verify the signature, anyone can apply the signer's public key and recover the hashed document. They can then calculate the hash of the document and compare it with the hash of the document that was signed. If the two values match, then the identity of the signer (as well as the ownership of the document) is verified. All of this hinges on the assumption that the signer's private key was not stolen or used against their will.

Digital certificate

Digital certificates are used to bind names to public keys. They certify that an entity owns the public key they claim to own. This binding is done by a **Certification Authority (CA)**, which verifies an entity is who they claim to be before issuing a certificate that binds the name and public key of the entity.

Generally, a certificate contains:

- the public key for the entity,
- unique information about the owner of the public key,
- a serial number for the certificate,
- issue and expiry dates for the certificate, and
- the digital signature of the CA.

Digital certificates are useful because they allow us to verify the public keys we see online. As long as you trust the CA that issued the certificate, you can be sure the public key for an entity actually belongs to said entity.

As you might expect, trust in digital certificates boils down to trust in the CAs. Therefore, a CA has extra incentive to protect its private key (which is used to digitally sign any certificates it issues).

The system for issuing, managing, and revoking digital certificates is (unhelpfully) called **public key infrastructure (PKI)**.

Email security: PGP

One of the most popular encryption programs around is PGP, which stands for **Pretty Good Privacy**. PGP can be used to sign and encrypt things like files and emails.

To get started, find and download a trusted version of PGP. Good examples can be found below:

- Windows: gpg4win.org
- Mac: gpgtools.org
- Android: guardianproject.info/code/gnupg
- iOS: ipgmail.com
- Linux: wiki.gnome.org/Apps/Seahorse and enigmail.net

The PGP software will help you create a public key and a private key. The public key can be freely shared, but you'll want to keep the private key to yourself. The private key is protected by a password, so be careful when choosing and maintaining your password. If you lose the password, you'll lose access to your private key too.

What can PGP do? Well, you can sign a file by applying your private key. Others can verify your signature by applying your public key to the signature. Or you can encrypt a file by applying a friend's public key so only they can read it (by applying their private key).

As useful as PGP is, some caution is needed. Since anyone can upload and share keys, you'll have to make sure a public key you're planning to use actually belongs to that person. PGP also received flak when vulnerabilities in email clients led to messages being decrypted. To defend against flaws like this, update your version of PGP regularly and make sure you haven't accidentally enabled any features you don't need (or disabled any that you do).

Cyberattacks

After exploring the basics of cryptography, encryption, and ways to validate messages and identity, we now look at some of the most common attacks on the Internet.

As we'll see, although there are a multitude of individual attacks on the Internet, many of them operate on the same underlying logic. We start with one of the most common: malware attacks.

Malware

Malware, as the name suggests, is malicious software that infects a host and performs unauthorized actions. There is a wide range of malware on the Internet, from **keyloggers** that record keyboard input to **ransomware** that locks your device (by encrypting all of its data) and demands payment to its creator. Here are the most common types of malware:

Virus

A **virus** is a piece of self-replicating code that activates or spreads with help from the host. Typically, a user needs to perform some action (e.g., clicking a link) to download the virus onto their device. Once a virus has entered a device, it inserts itself into other programs.

Worm

A **worm** is similar to a virus but can enter a host without user interaction. Worms do not need to attach themselves to another program. Rather, they self-replicate and spread through network vulnerabilities.

Trojan horse

A **Trojan horse** is malware that disguises itself as legitimate software. A Trojan horse does not replicate itself, but it is used to sneak malicious software onto a victim's device.

Defending against malware

There are several ways to defend against malware. A **firewall** can block unauthorized traffic and filter out packets that are deemed dangerous. We'll cover firewalls in greater detail later. **Antivirus software** can scan your device and remove malware. Since malware is always evolving, it's a good idea to periodically scan your devices and update your antivirus software whenever an update is available. Finally, an **intrusion detection system** performs more thorough packet inspection than a regular firewall and is often needed for more complex types of malware.

While all of these tools provide useful defenses against malware, common sense is also essential. Don't open suspicious links, don't visit sketchy websites, don't download anything from a source you don't trust, but do keep your software up to date. You can inspect a link by hovering your cursor over it. If you're on a mobile device, tap and hold (but don't let go too soon!) or copy the link into a text editor. Carefully examine the link for typos or unexpected characters before following it.

Denial of Service attacks

Denial of Service (DoS) attacks work by overwhelming a resource with bogus traffic, rendering the resource unavailable for legitimate users. When a DoS attack is carried out by a multitude of malicious hosts, it becomes a **Distributed Denial of Service (DDoS)** attack.

DDoS attacks are usually carried out by a **botnet**, which consists of a group of malware-infected hosts. Botnets are directed by a bot controller.

DNS flooding attack

An example of an application-layer DoS attack is a **DNS flooding** attack. Here, the attacker sends a large amount of bogus DNS queries, overwhelming the DNS servers and preventing legitimate DNS requests from being serviced.

Defending against DNS flooding

If all of the bogus DNS traffic is coming from the same source, an upstream router can block the traffic from the attacker and keep the DNS server available for legitimate DNS requests. These days, most servers also limit the amount of resources available to each visitor to prevent abuse from bandwidth-flooding.

SYN flooding attack

A **SYN flooding** attack follows the same principle as a DNS flooding attack, but instead of sending DNS queries, the attacker initiates a deluge of TCP handshakes by flooding the target server with SYN segments and not completing the handshake process. The hope is that all of the server's resources are exhausted by these bogus SYN messages, shutting out SYN requests from legitimate users.

Defending against SYN flooding attacks

SYN cookies help servers defend against SYN flooding. When a server receives a SYN message, it sends a SYN-ACK packet with a hashed sequence number (the "cookie") to the client. The server then forgets the cookie and doesn't allocate resources to the SYN request. A legitimate client will return an ACK segment with an acknowledgment value that is one plus the hashed sequence number. Once the server receives and verifies this ACK segment, it can then safely open a connection with the client.

Ping flooding attack

On the network layer, a **ping flooding** attack happens when an attacker floods the victim's network with ICMP (Internet Control Message Protocol) echo, or ping, requests.

Defending against ping flooding attacks

To defend against a ping flooding attack, you can configure your firewall to block pings from outside your network. Note that this does not stop internal attacks and may leave you unable to diagnose issues in your network. Alternatively, you can disable ICMP functionality on your router. This can be quite troublesome to perform and will also prevent you from running certain network diagnostic functions.

DDoS attacks

So far, we've assumed the attack comes from a single attacker. Things get trickier in a Distributed Denial of Service attack, where multiple attackers (often a botnet) overwhelm the victim with enormous amounts of traffic. Since a botnet usually includes thousands of hosts sending traffic at the same time, it is very difficult to identify and block each host in the botnet.

While there is no bulletproof way to defend against botnets, here are a few possible approaches:

- Firewalls and packet filters can be used to block suspicious traffic patterns.
- Scale up the number of available servers. This tends to be very expensive.
- The cache in intermediate servers can be used to satisfy legitimate queries and lessen the impact of the DDoS attack felt by end users.

- There are services that can divert traffic from a target's servers and "scrub" the traffic, so only legitimate traffic reaches its intended destination.
- You can try to identify the bot controller and block its IP address. However, it's not difficult for a blocked bot controller to move to a new IP if needed.

In general, it's hard to stop a DDoS attack at the source. To avoid falling victim to one, server or site owners should make the attacker commit more resources, to the point that it's not worth the effort to launch an attack.

Malicious code attacks

Before the Internet, developers only had themselves to blame for bad code. Nowadays, network administrators and site owners have to deal with malicious code from end users, who can wreak havoc with a few lines of input.

Cross-site scripting attack

Cross-site scripting (XSS) is one of the most common attacks on the Web. An XSS attack happens when an attacker submits malicious code to a site, which is executed during another user's session. For example, a blog visitor can post HTML and JavaScript code in the comments section that, when executed, lets them access the website's cookies and steal user credentials.

Defending against cross-site scripting

One of the simplest ways to prevent cross-site scripting attacks is to **validate** user input. Do not allow unnecessary characters or input that may be used to form malicious code. Even after input is submitted, employ double-check validation on the server before the information is stored in a database.

Another important step is to **sanitize** user input before it leaves the database. In practice, this means using a function like "htmlentities" to remove HTML markup, converting the code into a harmless string. The process of converting user input into a string of safe characters is known as "escaping" user input.

Finally, it's a good idea to limit where user-generated content goes. This means only inserting content from trusted users onto approved parts of the site's template files. Content from untrusted sources should be displayed only as text.

Cross-site scripting (XSS) attack

SQL injection attack

SQL injection attack

Like a cross-site scripting attack, an **SQL injection** attack takes advantage of poor input filtering to introduce malicious code into a site's servers. But where an XSS attack primarily uses HTML and JavaScript to attack other web users, an SQL injection attack uses SQL (the standard database query language) to steal information from a database or destroy it.

Defending against SQL injection

Due to the similarities between SQL injection and XSS attacks, the same principles of **validating** and **sanitizing** user input apply when defending against SQL injections. The good news is most SQL frameworks already include these functions.

Another approach, unique to dealing with SQL injections, is to use **parameterized queries**. A parameterized query is a query (i.e., a data access request) in which placeholders are used for parameters. The placeholders are only replaced by actual values at execution. This eliminates attempts to sneak in malicious commands through user input.

Spoofing attacks

Spoofing attacks happen when an attacker pretends to be a normal network user or device and uses false information to attack legitimate entities.

DNS poisoning attack

In a **DNS poisoning** attack, an attacker asks the DNS resolver to resolve a hostname that isn't stored on the server. The attacker then sends spoofed replies that map the hostname to a malicious IP address. If the server accepts the mapping, any legitimate users requesting that hostname will be fed the attacker's malicious IP address.

DNS poisoning attack

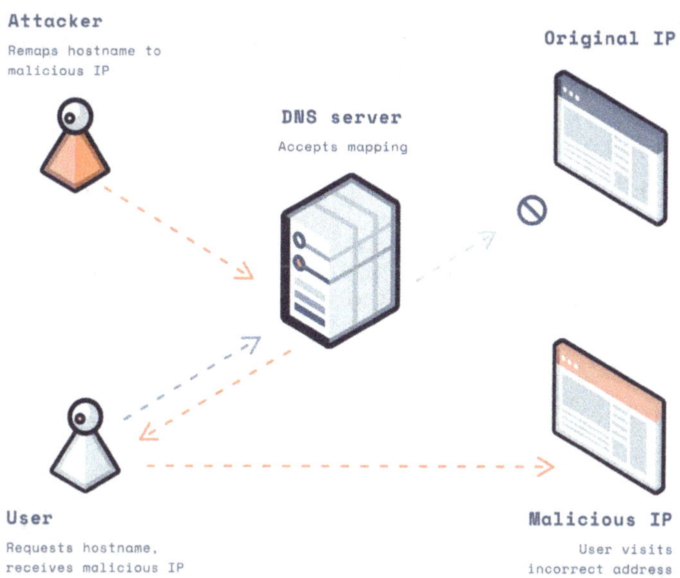

Defending against DNS poisoning

Fortunately, DNS poisoning attacks tend to be hard to execute. They depend on factors such as the attacker successfully guessing port numbers and often require a DoS attack to the DNS server to prevent legitimate replies from arriving before the attacker's spoofed replies.

If you are running your own DNS server, one easy approach is to simply block Internet DNS queries (over port 53) or to make your resolver private and available only to hosts in your network.

Man-in-the-middle attack

A **man-in-the-middle (MitM)** attack happens when a client is tricked into opening a transport-layer session with an attacker, who then opens a session with the server.

This "man in the middle" sits between the client and the server, who each believe they're directly communicating with the other. The MitM attacker can then intercept or modify communications, including any confidential information, between the two endpoints.

Man-in-the-middle (MitM) attack

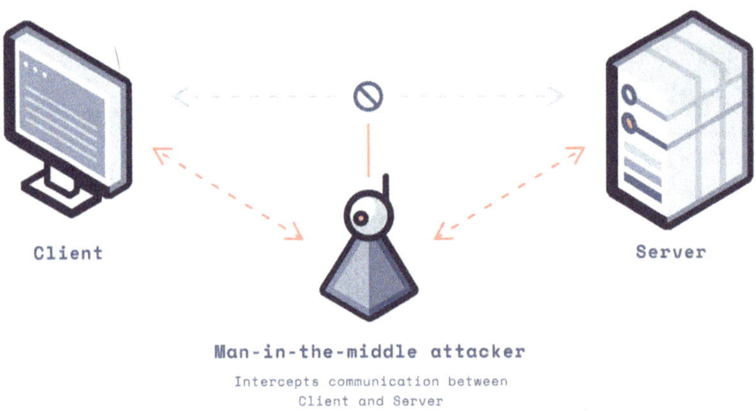

Defending against MitM attacks

To protect yourself against MitM attacks, avoid connecting to the Internet via public Wi-Fi hotspots. This is especially true if the network you're trying to use does not have a trusted SSL certificate. You'll usually be notified of suspicious certificates by a dialog box like this:

SSL certificate not trusted

The security certificate for this network is not from a trusted authority. We recommend that you do not connect to this network.

CANCEL CONNECT

In addition, avoid sites that run only on HTTP (instead of the secured variant, HTTPS) and make sure you enter URLs correctly to avoid being taken to a fake site. Finally, you can encrypt your device traffic by using a trusted and secure consumer VPN service, which we'll go into later. This is a good idea if you really need to connect to public Wi-Fi or visit a non-HTTPS site.

IP spoofing attack

IP spoofing attacks happen when an attacker sends IP packets with a spoofed source address. By hiding the true source of the packets, an attacker can trick the victim into accepting these spoofed packets.

IP spoofing is often used in DoS attacks. The attacker can directly overwhelm the victim with spoofed packets, or use the victim's IP address as the source address. In this second scenario, the attacker will send spoofed packets (with the victim's IP address as the source) to all manner of recipients, leading them to flood the victim with response packets.

Defending against IP spoofing

It's hard to defend against IP spoofing in the IPv4 space, as there is no reliable protection mechanism for the source and destination fields in the packet headers. IPv6 offers encryption capabilities (using IPsec) that would, in theory, eliminate IP spoofing. That said, IPv6 adoption has remained slow.

Until things pick up on that front, other measures include using a packet filter to block suspicious traffic and setting up an access control list to regulate who can interact with your network. Of course, these mechanisms won't stop attackers from faking the source address of packets, but they allow you to react and protect yourself if you're receiving a lot of strange traffic.

ARP spoofing attack

ARP maps IP addresses to MAC addresses. In an **ARP spoofing** attack, an attacker sends fake ARP messages that link a victim's IP address with a MAC address controlled by the attacker. Once these messages are accepted, data intended for the victim is sent to the attacker instead.

Defending against ARP spoofing

You can check if you're suffering from ARP spoofing by reviewing your IP-MAC address mapping. If you see a MAC you don't recognize or if an IP is "flip-flopping" between two MAC addresses, you might be dealing with an ARP spoofing attack.

A modern switch can be configured to prevent (or at least detect) ARP spoofing, but this feature is not commonly available on home switches. There are two other things you can do to defend yourself against ARP spoofing. Each comes with its own caveats.

First, you can use a VPN to encrypt your device traffic. It's important to note a VPN doesn't actually stop ARP spoofing—it simply encrypts packets so they can't be read by an attacker who captures packets from your network.

To "properly" defend against ARP spoofing, you can create static ARP entries for every machine on your network. This leads them to ignore ARP replies, including bogus ones. Unfortunately, static ARP entries only work against simpler forms of ARP spoofing and tend to be a pain to set up.

Social engineering

Easily the least technical of cyberattacks, **social engineering** simply refers to scams executed through human interaction. **Phishing** is a form of social engineering where the perpetrator tricks the victim into giving up confidential information. Scam emails and fake websites are often used by fraudsters to phish information out of unsuspecting victims.

While you can configure your email service to block spam emails, the best way to defend against social engineering attempts is to use common sense. It's impossible to win a contest you didn't enter, and if the heir to some multibillion-dollar estate needed someone to hold onto their money, you're likely not the first person they'd think of.

Also remember that no legitimate bank or service provider will ask you to submit your account credentials over an email. If in doubt, call the party in question (make sure you call their actual number!) or use a trusted search engine to visit their official website. If you're typing a URL, make sure you don't misspell it to avoid winding up on a counterfeit site.

Other security measures

In the previous section, we looked at some of the most prevalent forms of cyberattacks. You may have noticed a few defensive mechanisms repeatedly mentioned as countermeasures. Here, we consider how some of these tools work.

While it's impossible to find a silver-bullet solution that can stop every possible form of cyberattack, a general defensive principle is to create a setup that requires the attacker to spend more resources than what they would gain from executing the attack.

TLS (and SSL)

By default, TCP and UDP don't offer any encryption. This means any data sent over the Internet can be intercepted and modified. An obvious solution is to introduce encryption on top of the transport layer.

Transport Layer Security (TLS) (along with its predecessor, **Secure Sockets Layer (SSL)**) is a security protocol that's implemented in the application layer, on top of TCP.

In addition to a handshake protocol, TLS features a cipher suite to ensure messages are protected with approved security parameters. The cipher suite also has an alert protocol that notifies the receiver when a connection will be closed or if an error has occurred.

When used with TLS, unsecure HTTP web traffic becomes encrypted HTTPS traffic. TLS can be used by any application that runs over TCP, but each application has to "ask" for security and may have to undergo code changes to enjoy TLS encryption.

IPsec

As its name suggests, **IPsec** offers security at the network layer. Unlike TLS, IPsec automatically encrypts all data from the network layer and above. Individual applications do not have to "ask" for security.

There are two flavors of IPsec protocols: The **Authentication Header (HA)** and **Encapsulation Security Payload (ESP)** protocols. Both provide source authenticity and data integrity, but ESP also looks after confidentiality.

Firewall

A **firewall** is a combination of hardware and software that controls what traffic can enter or leave your network. There are two main types of firewalls:

Packet filters examine the content of data packets before deciding whether they can be permitted to pass. Typically, a packet filter will examine fields like the source and destination IP address, protocol type (e.g., TCP, UDP, ICMP, etc.), and source and destination port. **Stateful packet filters** go beyond examining individual packets and can track each stage of a TCP handshake. This makes them a more nuanced solution than traditional packet filters.

Application gateways are the other major type of firewall. Operating at the application layer, an application gateway looks beyond IP/TCP/UDP headers and examines data for a specific application. This is known as deep packet inspection and offers more "tailored" security coverage than a packet filter. Each gateway is application specific, so you will need one for each application you want to examine.

IDS and IPS

An **intrusion detection system (IDS)** performs IP/TCP/UDP header inspection (like a packet filter) as well as deep packet inspection (like an application gateway). Alerts are raised if there are anomalies in the observed traffic (compared with a "normal" traffic profile) or if certain known attack signatures are detected.

An **intrusion prevention system (IPS)** performs the same function as an IDS but also offers the ability to filter out and block suspicious traffic.

VPN

A **virtual private network (VPN)** is a private network that's configured over a wider network (like the Internet). It is a "virtual" private network because the private network actually uses a public network as its backbone. That said, VPNs are private because they use encryption to create a secure "tunnel" between you and the network you want to access. When you use a properly configured VPN, no one can see the data you send over the tunnel.

Depending on the VPN protocol used, the VPN itself operates on different levels of the protocol stack. PPTP and L2TP (which offer almost no protection) work on the data link layer, and IPsec on the network layer; OpenVPN can be used on both layers but typically operates on the network layer.

Corporate VPNs

Historically, the term "VPN" refers to corporate VPNs, which connect an employee to a company's network (or a branch office to headquarters). With a corporate VPN, an employee is privately and securely connected to the company's network and can access company resources as if they were using an office machine.

Consumer VPNs

Consumer VPNs have become popular over the last decade or more and can be used by anyone looking for online security and privacy. With a consumer VPN, the consumer first connects to a VPN server (via their ISP). The traffic between the client and the VPN server is encrypted, so the ISP can't inspect the traffic that's sent to the VPN server.

When the traffic leaves the VPN server and travels across the Internet, it is decrypted and can be seen by others. This is done because the destination for your traffic cannot decrypt the VPN server's encryption, so measures like HTTPS are still necessary even if you're using a VPN. To the receiver, your (decrypted) traffic appears to have originated from the VPN server, so your real IP address is hidden.

Connecting to a consumer VPN

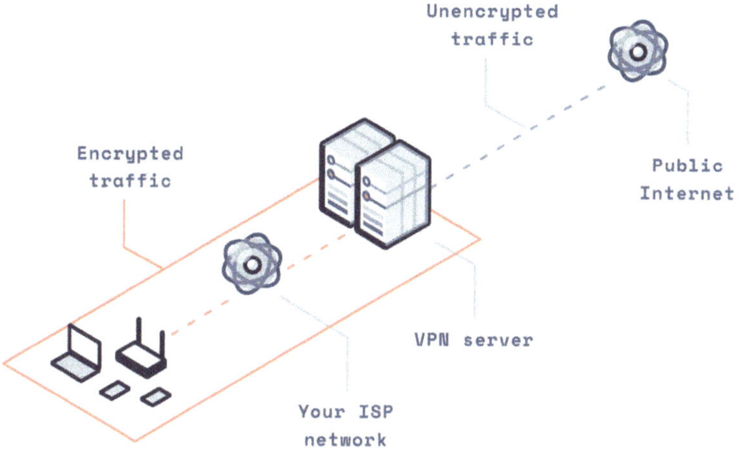

Does a consumer VPN make you completely "invisible" on the Internet? Hardly. Your traffic is hidden from your ISP and potential attackers, but service providers like YouTube can still identify you if you sign in to your account. YouTube would not know where you're signing in from, but if you watch a video, it would be able to track your activity via its own analytics. Using a VPN also doesn't protect you from malware. The best defense against that is using a combination of firewalls, antivirus software, and your own common sense.

5

Blockchain and Web 3.0

Up to this point, we've primarily looked at a very traditional, "client-server" model of the Internet. Although this is how most of the world currently uses the Internet, there are a few flaws with this model:

- **Centralized points of failure**. For example, a DDoS attack on an organization's servers can render its website inaccessible and cost them millions in lost revenue.
- **Centralized control**. The modern Internet is controlled by major "gatekeepers" and has resulted in a near monopolization of data (and value) under the control of a select group of companies.

Blockchain offers a new paradigm for Internet computing and is already changing the way information is stored and shared. But what is it exactly?

What is blockchain?

At heart, **blockchain** is a distributed database, made up of a chain of fixed-sized blocks. A block contains transactions, which are validated before they are added to the block. Each block also references the previous block using a hash function.

Blockchain is a type of distributed ledger, because each and every participant in the network has the same copy of the ledger. When this distributed model of storage is combined with encryption mechanisms, it allows distributed peers to store information and achieve consensus in a way that can't be easily compromised by bad actors.

As you may expect, essential to blockchain are the blocks and a mechanism to chain the blocks together. Blockchains also use two cryptographic components to identify participants, achieve consensus, and ensure the integrity of the chain:

- **Public keys** (for encryption and verifying signatures) and **private keys** (for decryption and creating signatures)
- **Hashes**

How does a blockchain work?

In simple terms, a blockchain transaction is hashed and then signed with the private key of the person who made the transaction.

Whenever a new transaction (e.g., T_1) is made, it references a previous transaction (T_0) to ensure the tokens used in T_1 are only passed on once. Namely, the new transaction references the hash of the previous transaction.

With this reference in place, T_1 is distributed to the network. Once it has been deemed valid, T_1 (and other new, valid transactions) will form the basis of a future block in the blockchain. A block is essentially an ordered list of approved transactions, a block header, and a hash of the previous block's header.

With this foundation in place, we can see how the blockchain is built. The first block is made up of transactions and a block header, while the second block will contain its own transactions, its own header, and a hash of the previous block's header. The hash serves as a "fingerprint" of the previous block, and is used to protect against data tampering as more blocks are added to the chain.

An illustration of the blockchain

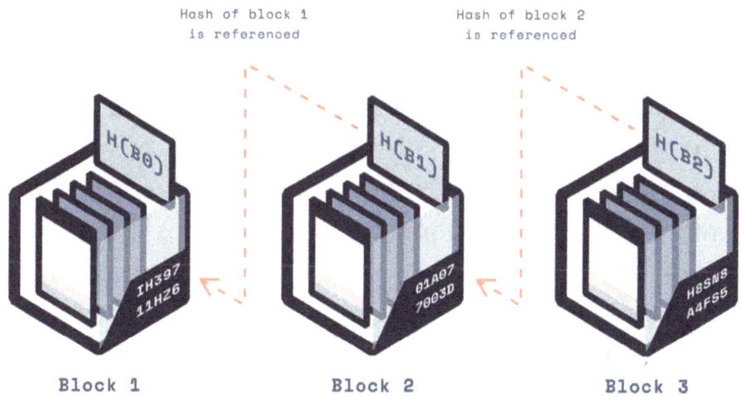

Extrapolate the example, and it's clear that blockchain makes it increasingly difficult to alter information as time goes by. An attacker would have to change a block and then redo all of the computations for subsequent blocks. Meanwhile, "normal" peers are processing and adding new, legitimate blocks to the chain. This makes it computationally (and economically) infeasible for bad actors to alter the chain of verified blocks.

Achieving consensus in blockchain

Remember that blockchain is a distributed database made up of a chain of ordered blocks. Given its distributed nature, how can peers agree what the next accepted block will be? This presents the need for a **consensus algorithm**—a set of rules for reaching agreement in a group of peers that may contain a few bad apples.

The two most popular consensus algorithms are **Proof of Work (PoW)** and **Proof of Stake (PoS)**. Besides these two, there are a range of other consensus algorithms used by other blockchain applications.

In a Proof of Work system, miners race to solve a complex mathematical problem for the right to select the next block. The problem involves finding a nonce (a number) such that the hashed value of the block header is smaller than some predetermined value. The only way to solve this problem is by brute-force guessing, so miners with higher computational power (perhaps by running more machines or more efficient machines) have a better chance of solving the problem. Because a PoW blockchain requires actual computational power, an attacker cannot simply run multiple instances of a server in an attempt to "outvote" honest peers and control the chain.

PoW blockchains also prevent cheating by allowing nodes to reject blocks that contain invalid transactions. Invalid blocks, such as those with an insufficient amount of work or those that do not contain the correct nonce, can also be rejected. When nodes reject the blocks, the blocks become worthless. In effect, this "forces" miners to only produce valid blocks and to not attempt double spending (see page 83). For all its benefits, Proof of Work is often criticized for its large power consumption and for damaging the environment.

In a Proof of Stake system, there are no mathematical problems to solve. Instead, the creator of the next block is selected pseudo-randomly, based on their stake. A stake refers to how many of the system's tokens the owner commits to not using for an amount of time. Naturally, the larger the stake, the more likely an owner is to be selected as the creator of the next block.

Unlike PoW, Proof of Stake does not have the same computational demands and discourages cheating in a different way. To control a PoS blockchain, an attacker must control enough of the available system tokens, which is often very expensive due to the limited supply of tokens. Bad actors that attempt double spends may also lose their stake and be removed from the pool going forward.

A challenge for PoS is the "nothing-at-stake" problem. In the case of a fork (where one chain splits into two), stakers are incentivized to work on both chains (because there is no cost to working on a chain but a potential loss if they end up working on the shorter chain). This risks endlessly splitting the chain, meaning there is no consensus over the current state of the chain. Hybrid consensus algorithms (like Decred) have been developed as one way to deal with the nothing-at-stake problem.

Blockchain in action: Bitcoin

If the Web is the most famous Internet application, Bitcoin is indisputably the most well-known blockchain application. Launched in January 2009, Bitcoin was the world's first decentralized cryptocurrency.

Although it's called a cryptocurrency, Bitcoin is not some virtual collection of coins that's transferred from one digital vault to another. Bitcoin wallets, commonly thought to be where Bitcoin is stored, actually don't contain any Bitcoin. So what exactly is Bitcoin?

Like the technology underpinning it, Bitcoin is, fundamentally, a chain of blocks. In this case, the blocks are composed of digitally signed transactions. Transactions are broadcast to everyone and stored on a public ledger. This makes it possible for anyone to verify the chain of Bitcoin transactions.

Bitcoin transactions

To transfer Bitcoin, the owner must digitally sign (with their private key) a message that has three components:

- **A hash of the previous transaction**. This proves the owner has previously received the Bitcoin they now intend to send to the receiver.
- **The amount of Bitcoin to be sent in the current transaction**.
- **The receiver's public key**. This is the destination the outgoing Bitcoin will be sent to.

Once the owner's digital signature is applied, the transaction is broadcasted to the rest of the network.

How Bitcoin transactions work

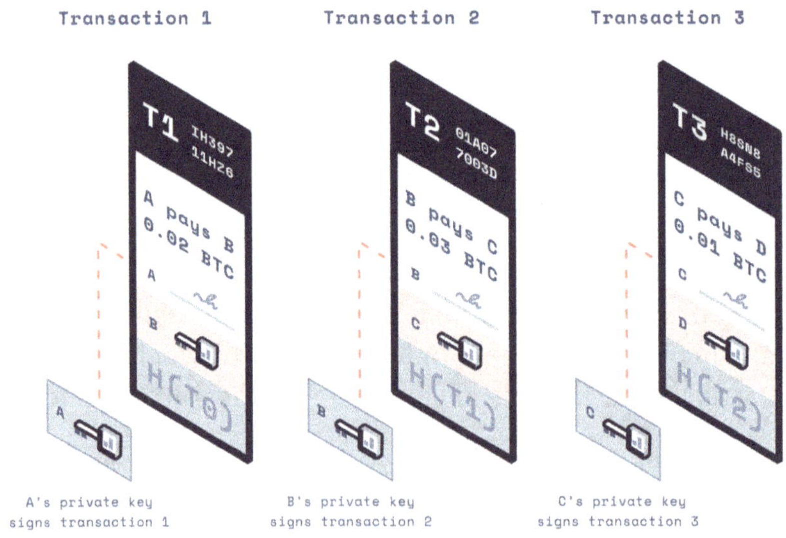

When it is first broadcasted, a transaction is "unconfirmed." To confirm a transaction, miners collect unconfirmed transactions into blocks of (unconfirmed) transactions. To complete a block, miners solve the PoW problem of repeatedly hashing a block's header (by changing the nonce value) until the resulting hash is smaller than some predetermined value.

Once a block is completed (i.e., once the miner finds the correct nonce value for the current PoW problem), it is transmitted to every peer in the network and the miner is given a reward. The block (and all of its constituent transactions) is considered permanent once it is followed (or "confirmed") by a sufficient number of subsequent blocks, with each block referencing its predecessor. To maintain a steady rate of block production, the difficulty for the PoW problem is adjusted every 14 days. The goal is to ensure a block is created roughly every 10 minutes.

You may be wondering, if there are all these chains that are constantly getting longer, which chain is "correct"? As a rule of thumb, Bitcoin peers accept the longest valid chain. This is because the longest chain is the product of the largest amount of computing power. In a network where miners are rational (i.e., profit maximizing), consensus will converge around the longest chain. This makes double spending infeasible.

Bitcoin and double spending

Another ingenious feature of Bitcoin is how it deals with double spending. With physical cash, there is no risk of double spending because you cannot spend a bill you just handed to someone else. With digital currencies, it's possible (at least in theory) to spend the same coins in a second transaction before the first transaction is confirmed.

If an attacker tries to spend the same Bitcoin in two different transactions, both transactions will be sent to the pool of unconfirmed transactions. However, as soon as one transaction becomes part of a confirmed block, the other transaction will be rejected and discarded. In practice, Bitcoin users wait for at least six confirmations (that is, for six blocks to be added to the block containing the current transaction) before accepting a transaction as valid.

Another way to attack the system is to wait for the first transaction to be confirmed before mining a contradicting block. In this scenario, the attacker has to build the contradicting block and get it confirmed by more blocks than the original block (to invalidate the chain containing the original block). While it's possible to pull off this attack with very little computing power, an attacker would need to be very lucky to sneak in a "bad" transaction in a network where they don't control the majority of resources. The attacker would also need to control at least 51% of available hashing power to execute the attack continuously and rewrite the entire chain. As mentioned earlier, a block is considered permanent after five or six confirmations. Any contradicting block will be rejected.

Other blockchain applications

Bitcoin may be the most famous blockchain application, but there are plenty of other useful applications that leverage this transformative technology. Here are a few:

Ethereum and smart contracts

Ethereum is a blockchain platform for building decentralized applications and executing smart contracts: contracts that transfer value when certain conditions are met. Unlike Bitcoin, which began life "only" as a cryptocurrency, Ethereum is a programmable infrastructure that was designed to support smart contracts.

The cryptocurrency used in Ethereum is **Ether**. Ether is used to pay transaction fees and is accepted as a means of exchange for assets on Ethereum. Ether can be bought, mined, or used as payment on Ethereum.

One of the most exciting uses of Ethereum is in the field of **decentralized finance (DeFi)**. Where traditional financial transactions (e.g., buying a car) require an intermediary (e.g., a bank) and trust in that intermediary, DeFi simply requires a smart contract to be deployed to Ethereum (or any other applicable blockchain platform). The code for the contract can be audited by anyone, and the contract will be executed if and only if the agreed-upon conditions are met. DeFi also does away with gatekeepers and unnecessary barriers to entry because anyone can create and use smart contracts. This leads to a more transparent and efficient system for all involved.

The public's interest in DeFi is not going anywhere soon. Over US$2.5 trillion of transactions was settled in the second quarter of 2021 on Ethereum, a staggering increase from the US$1.5 trillion settled in the preceding quarter.

Records management and non-fungible tokens

Identity and information management in the physical world is subject to problems like theft, loss, or forgery.

By providing a distributed ledger of verified records, blockchain purports to offer a solution to traditional records management problems. For example, the country and year of origin for a bottle of Chardonnay can be permanently recorded and made publicly available, protecting both the vintner and buyer. Sam's Club, a subsidiary of Walmart, undertook a similar initiative in 2020 when they partnered with a blockchain-based supply chain management platform to trace the food products sold in its stores. Industries as varied as banking, healthcare, and sporting goods are in various stages of exploring and adopting the technology.

The immutability of blockchain is central to another increasingly popular application: **non-fungible tokens (NFTs)**. To understand NFTs, let's first look at fungible assets, which are assets that can be readily interchanged. Banknotes are fungible assets because you can trade them while retaining the same value: If you trade a $100 note for another $100 note (or for two $50 notes), you'll still hold the same value of cash. Bitcoin is another fungible asset: You can split 1 BTC into 0.4 BTC and 0.6 BTC, and you'll still hold 1 BTC in value.

NFTs, by contrast, cannot be interchanged like fungible assets. They are digital tokens with unique properties that cannot simply be traded like for like. In practice, NFTs are used as ownership certificates for other digital assets such as a URL, a song, or an image. Anybody can visit a URL or copy an image online, but by minting an NFT (i.e., making a record on the relevant blockchain), a person can claim ownership of a digital asset. NFTs can be sold to new owners and can contain smart contracts that ensure the originator of the asset receives a cut from future sales.

Despite the rising popularity of NFTs, some have questioned whether it makes sense to issue "ownership certificates" for readily duplicable assets. To make matters worse, many of these selling platforms do not go to great lengths to ensure the minters of NFTs are the actual creators of the work. Many artists have reported seeing their work minted and sold without their permission. Lastly, there has been widespread criticism of the sizable energy consumption and environmental damage that comes from minting crypto art on PoW-based platforms like Ethereum.

Decentralized computing and Web 3.0

The "traditional" model of the Internet follows a client-server architecture. Under this model, clients request files from servers, whose job is to store files and satisfy client requests. Most data is stored in large data centers controlled by a handful of companies. Not only is it very expensive to run these data centers, but they are subject to downtime, security breaches, and the risk of centralized failure from DDoS attacks.

Decentralized storage and computing changes this paradigm by allowing any member node to act as a server. Users can offer idle computing resources for others to use (at a small profit) and enjoy large-scale storage and computation without the costs associated with a centralized provider. A decentralized infrastructure also makes it much harder for DDoS attacks to succeed. Enigma is an example of a decentralized computing platform powered by blockchain. Storj is an example of a blockchain-based storage platform.

As the world increasingly adapts to decentralized computing and storage, we move closer to realizing what's often called "Web 3.0." With Web 1.0 (a.k.a., the "readable" Web), the Web functioned as an information portal where site owners and content publishers "broadcasted" information for others to consume. Web 2.0 (a.k.a., the "writable" Web) follows the same client-server paradigm but allows users to interact with one another and publish their own content. With Web 3.0, we move beyond the traditional client-server model and into a decentralized Web (and Internet) that is powered by the ideals behind blockchain. This will reshape how people collaborate online and initiate major power shifts away from traditional central authorities.

The Internet of Things

Gartner previously estimated the number of connected devices to exceed 20 billion by 2020. As the Internet of Things (IoT) continues to grow, here are a few ways it can benefit from blockchain technology.

The first benefits are for identity management and security. The most valuable aspect of IoT is not the mere interconnection of millions of sensors. Rather, it is the vast deluge of data that is aggregated and shared by this multitude of devices. This includes the personal information of device owners and should be carefully protected. Blockchain, and the cryptographic mechanisms underpinning it, provides a powerful and tested way to secure this information against unwanted access or identity spoofing.

Another key benefit is scalability. As we've seen, a centralized infrastructure will always be at risk from concentrated points of failure. Blockchain, with its decentralized architecture, is better suited to handle the computing demands required for IoT to work at-scale and provides much stronger protection against DDoS attacks.

6

The Internet of Things and Cloud Computing

One of the biggest Internet buzzwords in recent years is IoT—the Internet of Things. Moving beyond a traditional network of connected computers, the IoT gives us "smart" devices that can "talk" to one another. By enabling all sorts of devices to communicate, the IoT gives us products like smartphone-controlled thermostats and fridges that order milk when we're running low.

In this chapter, we'll look at the Internet of Things as well as cloud computing, which is crucial for the growth of IoT beyond being a fascinating field in itself. We'll explore both concepts separately before seeing how they fit together.

What is the Internet of Things?

In simple terms, the **Internet of Things** refers to a system of interconnected devices, which can include objects as different as cars, TVs, refrigerators, and even clothing. The value of IoT lies in the vast amount of time-correlated data that is generated and shared by these devices.

Components of the IoT

Sensors and endpoints

The foundations of any IoT system are the sensors (or "endpoints") that collect data. Sensors take input (e.g., light, temperature, and pressure) and pump out data that can then be shared, aggregated, and analyzed.

Here are some common types of sensors used in IoT systems, along with two examples of each sensor type:

Types of IoT sensors

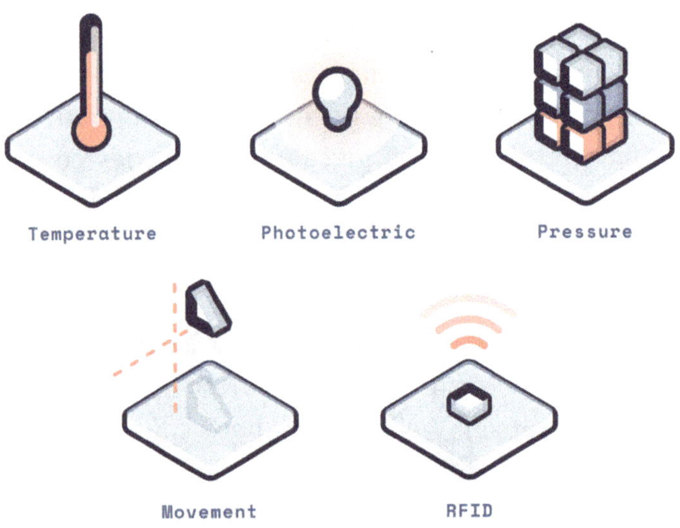

- **Temperature sensors**
    - Thermocouples measure temperature and emit a voltage corresponding to the temperature. Thermocouples can be found in water heaters and

ovens, where they perform the vital function of shutting the gas valve if the pilot flame goes out, to prevent excessive gas buildup.

- Thermistors generate electrical resistance based on the temperature. Thermistors are used in microwaves to maintain a constant temperature and prevent overheating.

- **Photoelectric sensors**
    - Photoresistors generate electrical resistance according to light intensity. Streetlights use photoresistors to "know" when to turn on and off. When the photoresistor in a streetlight is not receiving light (i.e., when it's dark outside), the light is turned on.
    - Photodiodes convert light into electrical current. Photodiodes are commonly found in smoke detectors, and generate a pulse that triggers the alarm when smoke particles cause light beams to scatter and hit the photodiode.
- **Pressure sensors**
    - Piezoelectric pressure sensors generate a charge when pressure is detected. They can be found in applications as varied as microphones and intruder alarms.
    - Strain gauge pressure sensors change resistance as pressure changes. They are used to measure stress on railway lines and airplane wings.
- **Movement sensors**
    - Accelerometers measure linear motion (or acceleration). They can be found in map applications and fitness trackers.

  - Gyroscopes detect rotational motion using gravity. These are typically used in airplanes and ships to assist navigation.

- **Radio-frequency identification (RFID) tags**

  - Active RFID tags use an antenna and microchip to capture and transmit data from radio frequency waves. Active RFID tags are battery operated and can be found in certain medical monitoring devices.

  - Passive RFID tags perform the same function as an active RFID tag but are powered by electromagnetic energy from an RFID reader. Passive RFID tags are commonly used in retail to track inventory levels and other product information.

Intermediate networks and protocols

Once data is collected at an endpoint, it needs to be transmitted over the Internet for computation and storage. Some of the most popular network technologies used include:

- **Non-IP-based WPAN**: Bluetooth and Zigbee (see Chapter 3). These technologies require significantly less computational overhead than IP.

- **IP-based WPAN**: 6LoWPAN. **6LoWPAN** stands for (deep breath) "IPv6 over Low-Power wireless personal area networks" and uses IPv6 addresses to extend IP communication to smaller, low-power IoT devices. 6LoWPAN creates mesh networks suited to the IoT and is the basis for another IPv6-based wireless personal area network, **Thread**.

- **IP-based WLAN**: Wi-Fi (see Chapter 3).

- **IP-based WAN**: 4G and 5G (see Chapter 3).

Besides new networking technologies, the IoT also requires new protocols for endpoint-generated data. HTTP, designed for classic client-server exchanges, is not ideal in IoT environments where bandwidth is often limited and devices are often much simpler.

The two most popular IoT protocols are:

- **MQTT (Message Queue Telemetry Transport)**: MQTT is based on TCP and uses a publish-subscribe model instead of a client-server model. Under MQTT, IoT nodes connect to a central broker and publish their own messages to the broker. They can also subscribe to the broker to receive messages for a certain topic (e.g., temperature). The broker subscribes to its serviced nodes and publishes messages belonging to a certain topic to nodes requesting that topic.
- **CoAP (Constrained Application Protocol)**: CoAP runs on UDP and follows a client-server model. A typical transaction begins with a CoAP client (or a proxy on behalf of the CoAP client) sending a request to a CoAP server. The server (or a proxy on behalf of the origin server) interprets the request and forms a corresponding response. If this seems very similar to how HTTP works, it's because CoAP is a HTTP-like protocol that's designed to consume less overhead and power. And where MQTT allows for one-to-many communication (via the central broker), CoAP was built as a one-to-one communication protocol that can be configured to support multiple recipients.

The Message Queue Telemetry Transport (MQTT) protocol

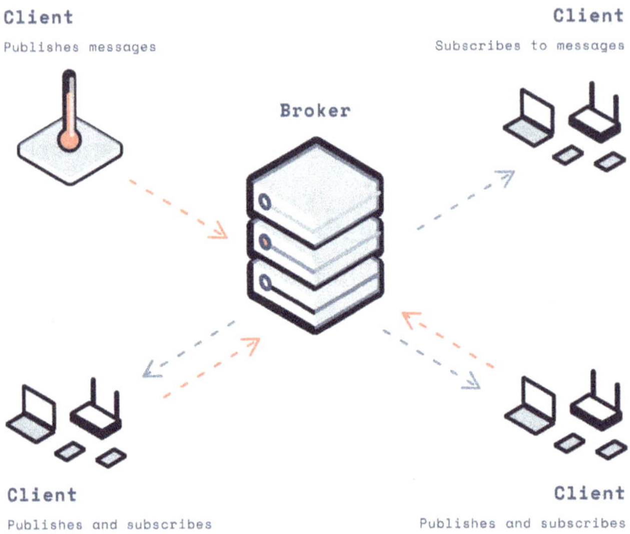

The Constrained Application Protocol (CoAP)

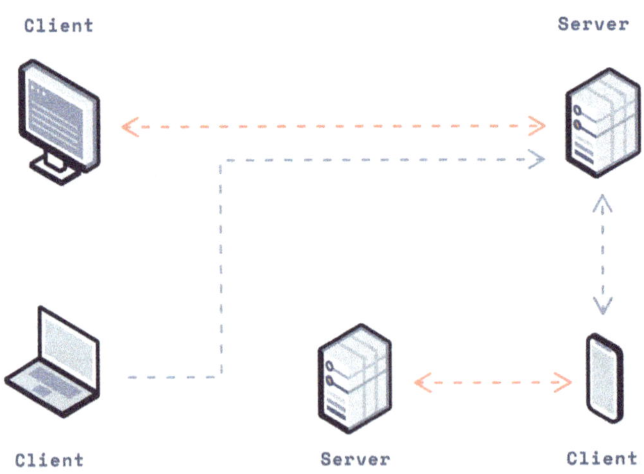

Cloud computing

The third component to IoT is the actual processing and storage of data. Traditional models of computing are simply incapable of handling the vast amounts of data generated and shared within the Internet of Things. Thankfully, the rise of cloud computing has offered a viable solution for the computational needs of IoT.

Put simply, **cloud computing** is a computing model where data processing and computational resources are made available over the Internet. In traditional models of computing, applications run on a hard drive or a local server. In contrast, a cloud is physically "manifested" in a remote data center (or several remote data centers) but gives the impression that the user is directly using the resource on their device. Besides offering services in an on-demand, "pay as you go" manner, cloud computing reduces the need for users to continually upgrade their hardware. You simply need a good enough Internet connection to use a cloud service.

There are three main "types" of clouds:

- **Private cloud**: The cloud and its resources are exclusively used by a single organization. However, the actual hardware (and its management) may sometimes reside with a third party.
- **Public cloud**: The cloud is owned and operated by a cloud service provider that offers on-demand cloud services to a variety of users.
- **Hybrid cloud**: This is often a combination of using both private and public clouds. A company may choose to use a private cloud for mission-critical activities and a public cloud for areas that require quick scalability.

Cloud computing models

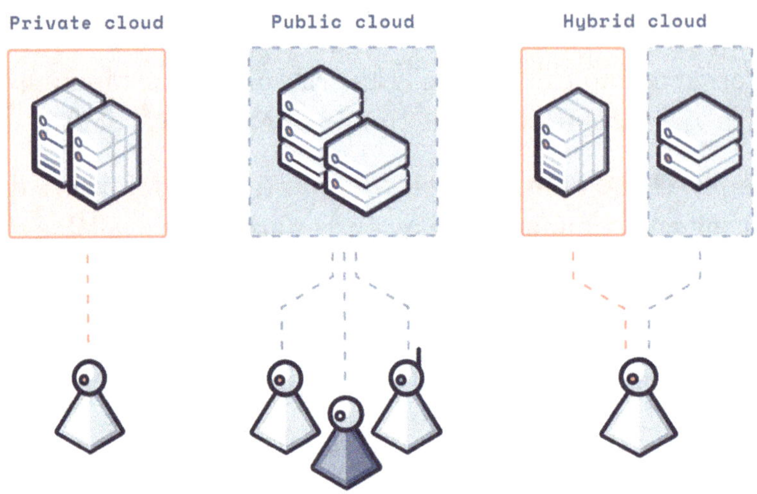

Another way of slicing cloud computing is by service model:

- **Software as a Service (SaaS)**: An application or service is offered on-demand over the Internet to customers.
- **Platform as a Service (PaaS)**: The tools for developing and maintaining applications are offered over the cloud.
- **Infrastructure as a Service (IaaS)**: Scalable hardware and virtualized computing resources are offered over the cloud for customers to run their own systems.

Google Docs (which this book was first written on) is a well-known example of a cloud computing service. When you use this public SaaS, your computer becomes the terminal on which you access the cloud-based word processor. Any data that's generated is saved on Google's servers instead of your computer. But to you, the user, it can sometimes feel like you're using an "old school" word processor directly on your machine.

Edge and fog computing

Unlike cloud computing, which moves data and processing to remote data centers, **edge computing** is about moving processing closer to the source of data, at the "edge" of the network.

At heart, edge computing is a concept about how computation should be done. The model that hews closer to reality is often called fog computing. **Fog computing** is basically a happy medium between cloud and edge computing: it is about allocating some tasks to the cloud-connected host and leaving the rest "in the cloud."

Voice assistants like Alexa, Siri, and Google Assistant follow this paradigm. When you say, "Hey, Alexa" to your Amazon Echo and issue a command, Alexa (running on your Echo) records and transforms your speech into code. It then determines whether it can satisfy your request locally or if it needs resources from the cloud (i.e., Amazon's servers). When it has the answer to your question (either computed locally or via the cloud), the response is "translated" into speech and played back on your Echo. This ability to perform some computing tasks on the "edge" (instead of doing it all "in the cloud") reduces the amount of waiting you have to do (and the amount of Internet bandwidth consumed) before Alexa answers your question.

The future of the IoT

Now that we've looked at the three "components" of the Internet of Things, what's on the horizon for this game-changing technology? Here are some exciting applications:

Transportation

The Internet of Things may not give us flying cars, but it is giving us connected vehicles that change the way we get around.

Embedded sensors and software can help drivers make smarter decisions and keep track of information like fuel levels and tire pressure. Connected cars will be able to detect each other, avoid collisions, and discover optimized routes based on real-time traffic information. Finally, connected cars have been shown to (literally) go the extra mile. In August 2019, Tesla disabled battery restrictions on their cars in response to Hurricane Dorian, allowing them to drive farther after one battery charge as gas stations ran out of fuel.

Healthcare and well-being

If you have an Apple Watch or a Fitbit, you already know how the IoT is helping us learn more about our bodies and take better care of ourselves.

That said, wearables only represent the tip of the IoT iceberg. Internet-connected pacemakers can help patients maintain a healthy heart rate and administer pulses as needed. Sensor-equipped wheelchairs can track a user's real-time location and call for help in emergencies. Insurers can also use health data from IoT devices to provide improved underwriting and claims processes.

Agriculture

The IoT revolution is also bringing substantial improvements to agriculture and husbandry. Internet-connected sensors help farmers keep a closer eye on the storage conditions of their grain, leading to a better and more sellable product. Cows can be tagged and have their eating patterns monitored, with the goal of rearing healthy cows that give the best produce. Smart tractors can also communicate with road vehicles and issue warnings to motorists when they are within half a mile of the tractor. Many other improvements to agricultural quality and safety are expected.

Workplace and industry

Finally, the IoT is also giving new meaning to the phrase "work smart." Smart bulbs can automatically adjust lighting levels based on the time of day or room usage. Connected printers can track ink levels and trigger refill orders when running low. A combination of sensors and tags can perform functions like detecting smoke, reporting congested meeting rooms, and keeping track of contractors doing maintenance work in the office.

In more industrial settings, IoT will popularize smart manufacturing (also called **industry 4.0**). Smart sensors will help factories reduce energy consumption and cut down on emissions, while the connection of previously "dumb" machines will allow for better control and planning of manufacturing processes. When combined with technologies like augmented reality, workers will also have access to safer and more precise production methods. These are a few of the benefits the IoT will bring to workplaces around the world.

A word on security

It's all well and good to embrace the benefits of the IoT, but there are caveats to consider as well. The most pressing concern is security.

With over 30 *billion* connected devices worldwide, the Internet of Things represents the largest attack surface on the planet. What's worse, most connected devices are simple in design and do not benefit from the same history of security upgrades given to personal computers and servers.

The stakes get higher when we look at the types of devices that are online. Hacked home surveillance systems can be used to plan break-ins, while a compromised pacemaker becomes life-threatening. The attacks we saw in Chapter 4 remain relevant, but a common denominator for IoT attacks is malware infecting unprotected devices.

A notably infamous example is Mirai, a malware designed to target Linux IoT devices. In 2016, Mirai infected around 600,000 IoT devices, creating a botnet, and launched a DDoS attack on hosting service providers like OVH and Dyn. Clients of these services, including Amazon, Twitter, and Reddit, became inaccessible to users. Although the creators of Mirai were arrested, the code found itself in the hands of other bad actors and new variants of Mirai continued to emerge in the next few years.

Besides Mirai, other examples of malware have crept into IoT devices and headlines around the world. In 2019, a 14-year-old created the Silex malware that bricked 4,000 IoT devices by exploiting known or guessable passwords. Once infected, the devices would have their storage emptied before ceasing to function altogether.

As IoT attacks get more complex and varied, here are a few things you can do to protect yourself:

- Make sure your IoT devices are using the latest software from the manufacturer and download any relevant patches (via trusted channels) when they become available.

- Don't use guessable passwords. Instead, randomize and periodically change them so they're harder to exploit. Don't hardcode passwords in ROM images.
- Close IP ports by default.
- Encrypt the connections on your devices. For example, if you're connecting a number of devices to a router, set up a VPN on the router (by configuring your own or by using a trusted provider) to protect every connected device.
- When a device is "retired" from your network, wipe all of the information from it and destroy the device before disposing of it.

A word on privacy

The value of IoT comes from the vast amount of data it generates. By collecting and acting on the data we supply, the IoT can provide "smart" services that are tailored to our personal needs. As we welcome more and more of these smart services into our lives, it's important to keep an eye on privacy.

In short, be aware of the permissions granted to each device or service. A fitness app may need to access certain body sensors on your phone, but it should not be accessing your contacts or modifying the contents of your device storage.

What's more, keep yourself informed about the service providers you're using. Many IoT devices from big companies have come under fire for intrusive behavior. Google stirred up controversy when it was revealed employees could listen to confidential phone calls and access domestic violence footage captured on Google Home. Another report found Amazon had hired thousands of auditors to listen to conversations recorded by Echo devices. Amazon's Ring has also provided camera footage to over 600 police departments in the U.S. While tech companies appear to be moving toward increasing transparency, the onus is on us to decide what data to share, and with whom.

A popular saying is that, on the Internet, "If you're not paying, then you're the product." In an IoT-centric world, we could be paying for devices that give away our data. The upshot of this is not to be distrustful of advancements in the Internet. Rather, it's a reminder to enjoy the benefits of this transformative technology with care and responsibility.

7

21 Questions about the Internet

To wrap things up, here are 21 questions that cover the purview of this book. It's intended to provide a handy summary of what we covered and jeopardize book sales because you no longer have to read the rest of the book. (Only joking. Please do read the rest of the book.)

1. What is the Internet?

The Internet is a network of networks, connecting devices around the world via a set of common protocols.

2. Who invented the Internet?

No one person invented the Internet. Leonard Kleinrock laid the foundations for packet-switched networks in 1961. Lawrence Roberts, building on ideas by J. C. R. Licklider, led the development of ARPANET, the predecessor of the Internet. Vinton Cerf and Robert Kahn invented the TCP and IP protocols that would define the architecture of the Internet. Paul Mockapetris introduced DNS in 1984, paving the way for Internet applications like the World Wide Web, proposed by Tim Berners-Lee in 1989.

3. Who controls the Internet?

No one has absolute control of the Internet. Rather, servers and computing resources around the world are owned by individuals, companies, and governments.

4. How does the Internet work?

The Internet works by having devices communicate over common protocols. Each connected device is given an address and uses that address when requesting and receiving information. The messages sent by devices are composed of bits (a one or a zero) and are broken into packets when they leave the sending device. They are reassembled into the original message when they reach their destination.

5. How big is the Internet?

Given its distributed nature, it's very hard to determine the actual size of the Internet. Back in 2013, the amount of information on the Internet was estimated to be around 3.7 zettabytes, which is a staggering 3.7×10^{21} bytes!

Experts predict the Internet doubles in size roughly every two years, and as of late 2021 the total amount of estimated data has exceeded 50 zettabytes. You can find a live tracker on www.live-counter.com/how-big-is-the-internet.

6. How much energy does the Internet consume?

Using figures from data centers, the U.S. Department of Energy's Lawrence Berkeley National Laboratory determined the Internet consumes around 70 billion kilowatt hours a year. For reference, 1 kilowatt hour is enough to keep a smartphone charged for an entire year.

7. What are the most important Internet protocols?

It's hard to narrow this down to a short list, but here are a few essential ones:

- TCP/UDP: Determines how data is transported across the Internet.

- IP: Provides an address for every host on the Internet.
- ARP: Finds the MAC address associated with an IP address.
- BGP/OSPF: Determines routing on the Internet.

DNS, which translates hostnames into IP addresses, is also an essential component of the Internet, but it's actually a distributed database that's implemented in servers.

8. Why was the Internet designed to be "stateless"?

The Internet was initially designed to be a simple, shared resource for trusted peers. Because of this, there was no need to maintain "state" information across communication sessions. As the Internet opened up to personal and commercial use, there was a need for a user's information to be "remembered." On the Web, this is done by cookies, which are text files that record your behavior and can be used to provide a more personalized experience. Cookies can also be used for intrusive tracking or cyberattacks, so they should be managed carefully.

9. What are some principles behind the design of the Internet?

There are many principles behind the success and scalability of the Internet. Here are three that are examined in this book:

- Maintaining a "separation of concerns" in the protocol stack—so each layer can focus on one function and can be changed without affecting the others.
- Pushing computing complexity to the network edge to keep the network core uncongested.
- Making attackers expend more effort than it's worth to launch an attack.

10. What's the difference between the Web and the Internet?

The Internet is the infrastructure on which the Web runs. The Web is only one of many applications that run on the Internet. It's possible to have the Internet without the Web, but it'd be impossible to have the Web without the Internet.

11. What's a router? How's it different from a modem?

A modem brings the Internet to your home. It establishes a connection with your ISP and demodulates analog signals from the Internet into digital signals that a computer can understand (and vice versa). There are cable modems (that use coaxial cables and are provided by cable TV providers) and phone-line, DSL modems.

A router sends packets to where they need to go—it routes data from one network to another (using IP addresses). In most home settings today a router and modem are usually bundled into one device.

12. How would someone shut down the Internet?

There are two ways to physically shut off the Internet. Attackers can take down the power grids powering servers around the world or destroy the subsea and fiber-optic cables that carry Internet traffic. Outside of a natural disaster, both are very hard to do.

The other way to shut down the Internet would be to attack BGP (responsible for Internet routing) and DNS (resolves hostnames to IP addresses). Something along these lines happened in October 2021, when Facebook accidentally withdrew BGP advertisements to their DNS servers. As a result, Facebook's DNS servers continued to function normally but could not be reached by external hosts. This led to outages for Facebook's various services for over five hours.

Fortunately, the systems behind BGP and DNS are very well protected against external threats and supported by backups. Modern Internet infrastructure also features redundant connections that allow traffic to be dynamically rerouted if needed.

13. Can I be completely secure on the Internet?

No. There is an ever-growing number of exploits and cyberattacks on the Internet. The best defense is to make sure any Internet-connected device you own is regularly updated and protected by trusted software. Beyond that, use common sense when using the Internet and don't reuse passwords (especially guessable ones).

14. Can I be completely private on the Internet?

No. Certain proxies and VPN services can hide your IP address, but you can still be identified online if you sign into an online account or make a purchase with a trackable payment method like your credit card. Furthermore, location and device information can also be used to build a profile of you online. For a rough idea of how "unique" you are online, visit amiunique.org.

15. What's 1G, 2G, 3G, 4G, and 5G? When's 6G coming out?

These are generations of mobile networks. They began as analog networks (1G) and have evolved into digital networks that carry Internet data. A new generation of mobile technology is expected to emerge roughly every 10 years.

16. What's Web 1.0, Web 2.0, and Web 3.0?

Web 1.0 was known as the "readable" Web. Here, the Web functioned as an information portal for organizations to "broadcast" information out to consumers.

Web 2.0 is often called the "writable" Web. Web 2.0 follows the client-server paradigm and allows user-generated content and interactivity.

Web 3.0 is the "decentralized" Web. Powered by blockchain, Web 3.0 breaks the traditional client-server paradigm and moves toward a peer-to-peer model. Many expect this to introduce a more "open" Web that has fewer barriers to entry and shifts power away from traditional Internet gatekeepers.

17. How does blockchain work?

Blockchain is a chain of fixed-length blocks. Each block contains validated transactions and is considered "permanent" after it's been followed by a number of subsequent blocks.

18. What is Bitcoin?

Bitcoin is a blockchain application. It is a decentralized cryptocurrency designed by Satoshi Nakamoto and became famous for solving the double-spending problem.

19. What is the Internet of Things?

The Internet of Things refers to the huge system of interconnected devices around the world. With the IoT, it is no longer only computers and smartphones that are going online. Household appliances like thermostats and clothing items can now connect to and share data over the Internet.

20. What is cloud computing, edge computing, and fog computing?

Cloud computing is a computing model where data processing and computational resources are made available over the Internet.

Edge computing is a philosophy about computing. It proposes moving data and processing closer to the devices that generate data, at the "edge" of the network.

Fog computing exists between cloud and edge computing. Here, some tasks are allocated to the cloud-connected host and the rest is done "in the cloud."

21. What will the Internet be like in the future?

It's relatively straightforward to predict what Internet technology will be like in the near future. The harder, and more important, question is what that means for individuals and societies.

On the technology front, it's a given that Internet speeds will get even faster. These days, people are already streaming their favorite shows, shopping online, and talking to their friends on the other side of the world when they're on the move. Expect these behaviors to become increasingly commonplace as Internet access becomes faster and cheaper. Enhanced Internet speeds will enable connected, driverless cars to change routes in response to real-time traffic. Telesurgery will become safer and more prevalent, giving patients access to the best surgeons in the world (as long as they can afford it!). When we can download full movies in milliseconds, we may be reaching a stage where Internet speeds are already "fast enough" and there's no incentive (at least for the average consumer) to upgrade to something even faster.

The other obvious technological trend is the increasing pervasiveness of the Internet. To date, Internet access has largely been confined to computer and phone screens. Luminaries like Leonard Kleinrock project a future where the Internet "will be everywhere, available on a continuous basis, and will be invisible in the sense that it will disappear into the infrastructure." Kleinrock goes on to speculate we may soon be interfacing with the Internet via gesture, haptics, and holograms in addition to speech, which many are already doing. Others predict implanted human-Internet interfaces will let people gather vastly more information (in much shorter times) than previously possible and "directly" communicate with other "cyborgs." While the productivity and efficiency gains are intriguing, some are worried about a future where we cannot "unplug" from the Internet. On a more philosophical level, there are concerns about what it would even mean to be human in this always-connected, "post-human" world.

The "science-fiction" scenario above is not meant to make us pessimistic about the future of the Internet. Rather, it's a segue into a broader question: How will (or should) we coexist with the Internet as it continues to grow?

Part of the answer depends on who controls the future Internet. Experts are split on this topic, with one camp believing corporations will come out on top. Justin Reich, a research scientist at MIT, believes today's Internet giants will likely remain in their positions 50 years from now, taking advantage of their market power and regulatory capture to remain ahead. As big tech players grow bigger and find ways to get around regulations, smaller competitors may get stamped out or be relegated to development roles. User data will continue to be collected and exchanged as commodities, as everyday users trade their information for Internet access and convenience.

In the other camp are those who think governments will take ever greater control of the Internet as more societies become surveillance states. Besides normalized tracking of Internet activities, there may be increased weaponization of the Internet, whereby governments launch online attacks or spread disinformation against states or organizations deemed dangerous to the regime.

Regardless of who wins this tug of war, net neutrality (the principle to not favor or discriminate against certain types of Internet communications) may not be a thing for long. ISPs can be incentivized to favor traffic from partners while governments are likely to clamp down on communications that undermine their authority. As Internet users, we have the right to demand an Internet that abides by its original principles—to be an open portal for the exchange of knowledge and information.

In this spirit, many predict increased demand for decentralized, perhaps ad hoc, network solutions. Sasha Costanza-Chock, another MIT academic, is optimistic that advances in Internet technology will make it easy for people to afford high-speed Internet access in the future. She expects this development to erode the power of for-profit ISPs and traditional platform providers. Others, like Södertörn University's Walid Al-Saqaf, point to the emergence of alternative decentralized solutions (such as blockchain) as users demand a "free" and unrestricted Internet.

Ultimately, the most important questions about the future of the Internet are no longer security questions, but ones to do with policy and human decision-making. While we can expect new protocols to be designed with security in mind, the more pertinent question is whether security is achieved to the detriment of privacy. And as IoT automation matures and Internet-connected AI replaces traditional labor, how are we going to spend our newfound free time? There's still so much up in the air (or should that be the cloud?), but if ever there was a time to be interested in the Internet and to shape its future, it's now.

01A07
7003D
Hello
World

Further Reading

You've reached the end of this book, but I hope this only marks the beginning of a rewarding journey on learning about the Internet. Below is a list of books and articles I've found useful while writing this text. They cover, in varying levels of depth, the topics we've encountered in this text as well as others such as web development and digital forensics.

A Guide to Computer Network Security (3rd edition), by Joseph Migga Kizza

"Bitcoin: A Peer-to-Peer Electronic Cash System," by Satoshi Nakamoto

Bitcoin: Security and Privacy, published by ExpressVPN

Blockchain: A Practical Guide to Developing Business, Law, and Technology Solutions, by Joseph J. Bambara, Paul R. Allen, and others

Computer Networking: A Top-Down Approach (7th edition), by Jim Kurose and Keith Ross

Computer Security (3rd edition), by Dieter Gollmann

Designing the User Interface: Strategies for Effective Human-Computer Interaction (6th edition), by Ben Shneiderman

Digital Forensics, edited by André Årnes

Distributed Systems: Principles and Paradigms (2nd edition), by Andrew S. Tanenbaum and Maarten van Steen

E-Commerce 2020–2021: Business, Technology and Society, Global Edition (16th edition), by Kenneth C. Laudon and Carol Guercio Traver

"Everything You Should Know About Certificates and PKI but Are Too Afraid to Ask," by Mike Malone, Smallstep

Help Your Kids with Computer Science, published by DK

How to Build a Billion Dollar App: Discover the Secrets of the Most Successful Entrepreneurs of Our Time, by George Berkowski

HTML and CSS: Design and Build Websites, by Jon Duckett

Internet of Things for Architects: Architecting IoT Solutions by Implementing Sensors, Communication Infrastructure, Edge Computing, Analytics, and Security, by Perry Lea

JavaScript and JQuery: Interactive Front-End Web Development, by Jon Duckett

Learning PHP, MySQL & JavaScript: A Step-by-Step Guide to Creating Dynamic Websites (6th edition), by Robin Nixon

Managing (e)Business Transformation: A Global Perspective, by Ali Farhoomand

Networking All-in-One for Dummies (7th edition), by Doug Lowe

Wireless and Mobile Device Security, by Jim Doherty

Index

C

D

E

F

G

H

I

R

S

Y

Z

www.ingramcontent.com/pod-product-compliance
Lightning Source LLC
LaVergne TN
LVHW022228200926
848481LV00006B/2172